THE RIVER, THE ROCK, AND THE REDEEMED

The River, The Rock and The Redeemed

*A history of missions work in the
Luapula Province of Zambia, 1898-2012*

Robert Muir

JOHN RITCHIE LTD
CHRISTIAN PUBLICATIONS

40 Beansburn, Kilmarnock, Scotland

ISBN-13: 978 1 907731 74 7

Copyright © 2012 by John Ritchie Ltd.
40 Beansburn, Kilmarnock, Scotland

www.ritchiechristianmedia.co.uk

Typeset by John Ritchie Ltd., Kilmarnock
Printed by Bell & Bain Ltd., Glasgow

Contents

Acknowledgements

I am pleased to acknowledge the gracious promptings of Miss Cathie Arthur who was at Mambilima for 48 years, and her encouragement to write this account. It was her sincere wish that some historical record of the Mission should be made.

My grateful thanks to my friend Dr Bert Cargill for his capable work editing what I have written. He has kept me on track and skilfully recast many of my somewhat unusual sentences.

Many thanks to those who have supplied material from their personal experiences and records. These include:
Miss Cathie Arthur, Mrs Margaret Hatcher, Dr Martin and Naomi Cooper, Miss Joy Pope, Mrs Rosemary Attwell, Mr Jim Hopewell.

Also special thanks to Mr Graham Johnson, Librarian at the Brethren Archives, John Rylands University, Manchester, for making available material from these archives.

Thanks to the publisher John Ritchie Ltd., for producing this book in such an attractive format.

Lastly my deepest thanks to my wife Margaret for all her help and encouragement. Together we have enjoyed researching and recording these years past and present. Reminiscences like these have given us more reasons and occasions to rejoice together.

Foreword

The title of this book takes you to a special spot in central Africa where Robert and Margaret Muir have spent many days in the service of God, much of which has been described in his earlier book *You shall go out with joy.* This is a noble attempt at recording the eventful history of it all.

The **River** is the great Luapula which farther downstream becomes the River Congo flowing into the Atlantic Ocean after about 3000 miles. Before it reaches Lake Mweru its upper section forms the boundary between the present Democratic Republic of Congo and the north eastern section of the Republic of Zambia. At this point it is nearly half a mile wide, and the large village of Mambilima sits on its eastern bank just below spectacular rapids. This is the place where Dan Crawford crossed from Congo to establish a base for missionary work in 1898, and as you will read, this is where this story begins.

The **Rock** is no insignificant outcrop. Dominating a flat area along the river bank stands a huge brown boulder perched on so small a base that when you see it first you fear it could topple over and crush anyone sheltering underneath. But it has been there for thousands of years without moving. The rock is some 20 ft high and 35 ft in diameter, with an overhang facing the river, big enough to give 20-30 people shade from the hot Zambian sun. At this spot over the past 12 years a large conference site has been established, and the rock is the preaching point with a pulpit built under the overhang. Regularly many thousands of Zambian Christians gather round to listen to God's Word being taught for several days at a time. How they value the Word of God being explained to them, and what precious fellowship they enjoy over these days of conferences.

Those believers in Christ are the **Redeemed**, those whose forebears had never heard the gospel until it reached these parts just over a hundred years ago. They are now numbered among the millions who know they have been "redeemed to God by the blood [of Christ] out of every kindred, and tongue, and people, and nation" (Revelation 5.9).

This book traces out in poignant and effective language how this came about by the grace of God and through the faithfulness of many of His servants. Devoted to their Master they pioneered and persisted through bad times and good, through sickness, death and disappointment, until the light of the gospel dispelled the darkness of sin and cruelty and unbelief. Today what we call civilisation is only slowly catching up on these Zambians, but the gospel got there first. Hundreds of autonomous churches have been established throughout the region, where local men and women are now communicating God's Word to their own people and seeing the number of the redeemed increasing day by day.

Authentic and verified histories are hard to come by, and Robert Muir has done us a great service in researching, checking, and recording the development of this work of God in that region during the past 114 years.

On a memorable day in August 2008, four white couples stood side by side among 14,000 native Zambians and sang a beautiful hymn in the shade of that rock from which God's Word had been preached for several days. Looking towards the gently flowing Luapula River, over a sea of faces shining with the joy of the Lord they sang these words by Frances Ridley Havergal,

> *"Like a river glorious is God's perfect peace,*
> *Over all victorious in its bright increase;*
> *Perfect, yet it floweth fuller every day –*
> *Perfect, yet it growth deeper all the way."*

What a joy it was and is to observe and share the joy and the perfect peace of the redeemed of the Lord from whatever nation or background they have come.

I trust that as you read this fascinating book which I thoroughly recommend, you too will be enjoying that perfect peace. I trust also that we will all be able to appreciate along with Robert and Margaret how in that part of Africa and elsewhere, "other men laboured, and we have entered into their labours" (John 4.38).

Bert Cargill
St Monans
Scotland

Introduction

This book has been researched and written as a result of a challenge issued by Miss Cathie Arthur. She was anxious that the history of Christian work done by those known as "Brethren Churches"[1] in the Luapula Province of Zambia and particularly at Mambilima be recorded from the beginning. Looking at me straight in the eye with that look which said, "Are you going to do it?" I could not wriggle out of it!

So I have taken up the challenge and the task has proved to be bigger than anticipated. How does one condense 114 years of history into a small book? How is such a story to be told so that the reader keeps up with the writer? Can I tell the story in such a way that God is glorified and the efforts of so many of His servants properly acknowledged? I trust that by the help of the Lord these things have been achieved.

This is not an exhaustive history nor is it a complete record of all the missionary work in the province from 1898 to 2012. It is a selection from the material available, gleaned from books and articles published in journals, from communications by missionaries to Echoes of Service, and by listening to those who worked at or visited Mambilima.

The story will show some massive changes. It will move from a situation of heathenism and cannibalism where the name of Jesus Christ was not known, to a situation today where thousands love and worship Him as their Lord and Saviour. It will take us from a province where illiteracy was very high to one where the percentage of illiteracy is now very low.

The early days saw the forest cut back and undergrowth being cleared; eliminating leopards, lions, hyenas and other carnivores; also cutting timber, making mud bricks, and getting together all necessary building materials for dwelling houses and mission buildings. Today there is a large Mission compound on the site with a fully functioning hospital, a residential basic school and a high school for physically handicapped children, a large church building, a bookshop and reading room, and many staff houses.

In those early days it was necessary that the native authorities gave a welcome to visitors before land was granted to settle on. This permission was given by the tribal chiefs for the first missionaries to settle, and indeed to choose as much land as was wanted. In this way a large piece of land was secured for a mission station at Mambilima.

The medical and educational work which has been developed over the years has been much used by God to reach the community with the gospel. In the early days schools were commenced in the village and the surrounding areas, with the basics of reading, writing and arithmetic being taught along with the Word of God. From the beginning the love of God was shown by these works and eventually lives were changed.

But the early part of the story will tell how for many years the scriptures were taught to children and to men and women of all ages before any visible fruit or any outward manifestation of interest in the gospel was seen. Then the Lord moved in the hearts of the people, the Holy Spirit convicted people of their sin and many turned to Jesus Christ for salvation.

Since these days the work has grown and today there are over 400 CMML churches[1] in the province. The mission at Mambilima has had a big influence on the growth of this work. It has been a centre where people have come and gone, many having given years of service. Visitors to the mission have been numerous. A Visitors' Book from 1926 records hundreds of names, some staying for only a day, many others for a week or a great deal longer. It was a hub of great activity, so that from all over Africa and from across the world they came to this outpost on the banks of the Luapula River.

The author realises only too well that the book has many limitations. Inevitably names will have been forgotten or missed out. Some readers will wonder why this one or that one is omitted, but the numbers are so vast it is impossible to include everyone. What is certain is that each one who knew Mambilima has their own recollections of the experience, many loving it and others loathing it!

My hope is that this record will give a real flavour of what has happened over these 114 years as we have watched God at work. We trust it will glorify the Lord Jesus Christ as we observe His church being built in this area. We are simply grateful to have been a cog in a large wheel, and to have been used in some small way to move forward with God in His work.

May all who read these pages get as much enjoyment as I have had in researching and writing them. Our prayer is that God will use this record to stimulate and encourage some to get more involved in the work of the Lord.

Robert Muir
Cowdenbeath
June 2012

[1] The churches referred to in this way and throughout this book do not have a denominational affiliation or common group name. The name "brethren" which is often used comes from the fact that the members are brothers and sisters in the family of God through faith in Jesus Christ as Saviour. The initials CMML stand for Christian Missions in Many Lands, this derived from the manner in which these churches were first registered by the authorities in several parts of Africa. Each church is autonomous, led by local elders according to the teaching of the New Testament.

CHAPTER 1

The Beginning, 1897

Our story begins on 18th June 1897 at Luanza in what was then Belgian Congo. Following in the pioneering trail of David Livingstone and then Fred Stanley Arnot, Dan Crawford had left Greenock in Scotland and reached Africa in the year 1890. Now seven years later Dan Crawford and his wife Grace (nee Tilsley) are making preparations to visit the grave of David Livingstone far south at Chitambo. Staggering down the 300 feet high cliff at Luanza they reach the edge of Lake Mweru which separates Belgian Congo and Northern Rhodesia. With their goods and chattels they climb into dug-out canoes and off they go, a new adventure for them and their party, paddling slowly away into totally uncharted territory.

Their first stop after crossing the lake was the palace of the paramount chief, Mwata Kazembe. This man held great authority and wielded great power in what is now the Luapula Province of Zambia. The Crawfords were on speaking terms with this man and successfully negotiated permission to travel south through his territory.

The journey took them into swamp lands with many beautiful lagoons. Progress was slow while they explored the terrain. Here they met some of their Lunda friends lounging under the spreading cloth trees, their scant clothing made from the bark of these trees. The men wore a loin cloth and the women little more. The women cover their heads in beads, sometimes making fulsome caps. They smear their bodies with an oil which improves their looks, but oh, how they smell!

Grace describes the villages as having a public dining room. This was just an ordinary native hut minus the walls, the roof being supported on small poles. All the men must dine here together, as it was a crime for any man to eat secretly in his own house. In the etymology of the Lunda language, "criminality" has as its seed thought this crime of eating alone. The feeding arrangement is wonderfully simple; the men either all starve or they all feast! A slave too, as a rule, eats the same as the chief.

Grace notes that the villages smell of all that is ill. It is like living on a dunghill! To get near the people one has to reckon as dead all sensitivities and olfactory organs. The villages are numerous, wild animals are always around. Grace describes how they were attacked by a leopard, but by the grace of God managed to escape. Each night they find a little clean spot for snug, cool and clean sleeping quarters.

The style of the architecture is uniform throughout. Houses are built wholly of bamboo plaited together basket fashion, the roof covered with a wiregrass so very fine it is put on barely an inch thick. The chief builds in the centre of the village and is usually very snug, all the others building around him in any fashion they like. The result is a village built like a maze full of blind alleys!

Soon the party reaches Kashiwa's village. (This village now known as Kashiba is on the Luapula River and today is an official border crossing from Zambia to Democratic Republic of Congo.) Chief Kashiwa is described as an extremely nice man. He is going to provide a rest house where missionaries can stay when they pass this way.

The next day they reach Mulundu's village farther south and upstream. Chief Mulundu is throwing his weight around and trying to block their way. Although Chief Kashiwa is more senior to him he is making the point - he also is a chief in his own right! Don't we all like to be acknowledged as people in our own right? After extensive palaver the party are given an *insaka* (dining room) to make camp for the night.

This very place is the site of present day Mambilima (meaning "The Jumping Waters"), or Johnston Falls as it was then known. Here the deep boom of the Falls was (and still is) clearly heard day and night as the Luapula River thunders and boils over the rocks. The Falls are not high waterfalls but really an extensive set of rapids which cannot be negotiated by boat.

From this point the Crawfords move overland, going many miles south of Lake Banguelu to the marked tree at Chitambo where Livingstone died in 1873 and where his heart was buried. His body was taken to England and buried beside that of other great men in Westminster Abbey in London. On his tombstone is inscribed the verse of scripture which had motivated him to risk all for the African unknown: "Other sheep I have which are not of this fold: them also I must bring" (John 10.16).

On the return journey Dan and Grace Crawford arrive back at Johnston Falls. He recognises its strategic location and great potential for a mission station. Leaving again by canoe to complete their journey back to Luanza, he promises to return and begin a work here.

On September 14th 1897 Dan Crawford and Henry Pomeroy set off from Luanza and again travel south east towards the Falls on the Luapula. Crawford says, "It is now the 'white African winter', but it is the whiteness of a glowing furnace and as hot as an engine room."

As they near the Falls they discover that all the boats had transferred to the opposite bank. The local people had mistaken them for a Belgian army attacking party. Chief after chief had mustered men on the bank to resist the force. Then discovering who they were, they slunk back at eventide and gave them gifts of food.

Two couriers were rushed off to Kazembe's capital to explain to him why they had entered from the west. In the meantime they crossed the river and made Chief Mulundu thoroughly ashamed of himself. Crawford says, "Africans have strange prejudices as to direction." Entering a village from the wrong direction has on occasion meant death.

That next night at sundown Crawford crossed the river and killed a monster hippo. A great cry of joy went up from both banks of the river, drums began to beat and canoes came darting from all directions to do the ponderous work of cutting up. Now "where the carcase is, there are the vultures gathered together" – and in boats too! The many people gorge themselves in their most famished style at the consumption of this hippo! To quote "whose god is their belly" is probably appropriate, but it must not be forgotten that their monotonous diet of cereals creates a ravenous craving for meat!

Crawford reports how in this way he won over the whole area. Deeds are more effective than words - he had invited the whole tribe to dine with him. This is elegantly rendered in the Luapula alliterative proverb, "Brow of brass, but belly of butter". It was a curious way of capturing a tribe - camping on its utmost border and asking your enemies out to supper. The soup tickets were without money and without price! The net local cost of his four tons of hippo meat was the round sum of sixpence for a cartridge!

Crawford goes on to tell that on the 26th September they choose the site for the mission. It is hard by the British (Rhodesian) bank of the river – an island lying off in mid stream, nearly opposite. The sound borne in day and night is of water boiling, wheezing and thudding. The banks are of a healthy sandy sort. The view looking upstream is like a rugged monster made of pudding stones spread across the river forbidding passage to all boats, but a beautiful site for the arrival of boats from downstream.

The chiefs who yesterday were up in arms against Crawford are today eating out of his hand. Some who had been shooting poisoned arrows at the men come crawling towards them today. Kazembe has sent word daring any of them to do other than treat the visitors right royally.

On the 3rd October there was great excitement as the *Mutumwe Wa Imani* came into view. This was a schooner that had been rescued and had sailed upriver from Luanza. It was a beautiful sight as the mist covered the river and the red sun was just breaking into the sky. "Black and pink hippos, still abed on sand banks, crocs, too, in hundreds push off in sheer disgust at our approach. The last item and best – the masts of God's brave little craft rise over the bank, and we put on a spurt to meet her. We have proved this Luapula to be a fine navigable waterway as far as the Falls."

Crawford and Pomeroy having chosen the site for the mission left two boys to begin foundations for a house. On October 4th they hoisted the sail on *Mutume Wa Imani* and set off down the Luapula for Luanza. There was great rejoicing when they reached there on October 17th.

As promised, Mr Pomeroy and his boys set sail for Johnston Falls on 21st December. Unfortunately he had not got permission from Mwata Kazembe to build his house. The chief was upset that they did not ask his permission before they started to dig the foundations! Is this like present day Planning Permission? However he said he was still his friend and sent him an ox. But he is afraid to allow the British into his territory, and wary of being attacked by white men, that is why he will not allow them to build in his country.

Mr Pomeroy was therefore obliged to cross back over to the Belgian side of the Falls where Chief Chisamba lives, and set up camp there. Here he lived until permission was granted to build at Johnston Falls. Eventually in 1898 the work commenced, a work that would have far reaching consequences to this day.

Dan Crawford, *Konga Vantu*, "Gatherer of the People"

CHAPTER 2

Gaining a Foothold at Johnston Falls

Henry J Pomeroy received permission to settle in Johnston Falls in 1898. It was a very troublesome time and attempts were made to kill him with poisonous arrows frequently shot at him, and his house burnt down. The Mwata Kazembe (the Paramont Chief) was the instigator of such attacks, but God spared Pomeroy's life and he persevered to try to gain the confidence of the people.

Mr and Mrs Anderson soon joined him in the work. Mrs Anderson was Mr Pomeroy's sister, and together they started to create a bridgehead for the gospel. They first spent much time and effort trying to make the place suitable for living. Wildlife was abundant, roaming the thick, dense undergrowth. The mosquitoes were vicious and Mr Pomeroy had repeated attacks of fever which left him weak. Eventually he was incapacitated by sunstroke and he had to give up the work in 1899. Later on, in 1924 he married Miss Frances Handford and they went to Algeria. Eventually they settled and worked in northern Nigeria.

The Andersons continued the work for a time until they too fell ill. During this time the political situation in the country was changing. In 1899, in conjunction with Robert Codrington (Acting Administrator for North-Eastern Rhodesia), Alfred Sharpe sent in British officers with troops who burnt Mwata Kazembe's capital to the ground, killing a number of his people, although Mwata himself had already escaped across the river.

This great Mwata Kazembe X made his way south and crossed back over the river to take refuge in the Johnston Falls Mission. Now he was in the place he had opposed, seeking refuge from the people he had tried to kill two years earlier. How would the Andersons respond in this situation?

Their Master had taught "if your enemy hunger feed him", and this is what they did. More than that, Mr Anderson looked after Mwata's men at Johnston Falls. Then Mrs Anderson took Mwata Kazembe on his own to the British Officers at his burnt-out capital. "Please be kind to him," she pleaded. Disarmed by this approach, and by the Mwata's agreement to accept their rule, the British agreed to let him come back. Mr Lammond was later to write that one of the officers involved had reported to him, "What else could we do with the man when a woman brought him by the hand and said, 'Do be kind to him'?"

Sadly, ill health drove the Andersons home also, and for a time the voice of testimony fell silent. Then in 1900 Mr Dugald Campbell crossed over from Katanga and built a permanent mission station there.

Dugald Campbell was an illustrious Scot who visited Africa around 1871 and then returned in 1898. By this time he was married to a lady who had studied medicine and midwifery at Queen Margaret College in Glasgow with the mission field in mind. After a hazardous journey from Bihe to Katanga, and later across the Kundelungu mountains, they entered the lion infested Luapula valley at Johnston Falls. This was no tourist journey with a three month old baby and wars and slavery to right and left.

This restarted the work at Johnston Falls which Mr Pomeroy and the Andersons had left because of illness. It would be the start of much real adventure. The area is very attractive for two reasons. Firstly the soil is rich and fertile, and secondly the river abounds with fish and the plains with game. So it is heavily populated with less fluctuations than in other parts, creating a more stable centre for a permanent work. It was a new field and so far there had been no conversions.

Campbell crossed over the Luapula to the site on which he would settle in spite of the danger of bringing his wife and child into a situation where a smallpox epidemic was raging. They built a camp and got going. Soon trees were cut down, the dense tangled bush that hid lions, leopards and buffalo herds was cleared. Anthills were dug and puddles made to get clay for bricks. Timber was sawn for doors and windows.

Two leopards were shot on the spot, a dozen hyenas were poisoned, and there were several escapes from lions. Buffalo and other game filled the pot for the workmen. One of the anthills they dug happened to be a cemetery and skeletons came to light! But the work went on.

At Johnston Falls he now found an open door - the welcome he received was more like a reception. Permission had been given to settle, and freedom given to have as much land as he wanted. Plans were made for the start of several buildings, vegetable gardens were laid out and fruit trees planted.

A house and a school hall which held 350 were erected. This was filled to overflowing on a Sunday. Two church services were held every day, and school three times a day. Soldiers, government servants, and chiefs along with men, women and children attended the schools and services. A sound foundation was being laid for a future work. Schools were simple with the aim of seeing the salvation of souls and growth of Christians. Intelligent reading and understanding of the Scriptures, writing in a plain hand to encourage correspondence, and instruction in elementary arithmetic were the basic curriculum.

Campbell describes how he dealt with a smallpox epidemic. Because of the lack of lymph for vaccination they borrowed a notion from the Arabs. Pus was taken from the ripe pustules of an infected person and lightly rubbed into a wound made in the skin of a healthy one. He does not record the success rate! During an epidemic of dysentery people were greatly helped by administration of caster oil and chlorodyne. Famines occurred regularly and for food they depended on his skill with the rifle.

The sandy beach on the river and the rock-strewn falls nearby at that time were filled with crocodiles, their mouths gaping wide while little birds raced about inside picking clean their foul teeth. They would often hide and grab an unwary traveller, or seize a woman drawing water. Canoes lined the riverbank. Fishermen went out at night with torches alight to drive fish into their cleverly woven nets.

Before government occupation, many witches and wizards had been tried and condemned by the poison test or the boiling pot ordeal. Many had been executed by tribal law for practising lycanthropy, saying they possessed the power to enable them to change into lions, leopards, crocodiles and such like. This belief can still be found today in certain areas, and personally I have heard a man tell how he changed into a cat and climbed up a tree. This belief can still be found even among those who confess their faith in the Lord Jesus Christ.

Stories abound from this era of men fighting lions, leopards and crocodiles, killing them with only an axe or a knife.

Others slew buffaloes, hippos, and elephants with long-shafted spears or harpoons.

It was into this country at this time that the great message of the Lord Jesus Christ began to come, and now He has become the Christ of African lakes and rivers.

CHAPTER 3

The First Conversions

For years Campbell laboured and preached the Gospel without any visible fruit or any outward interest in the Word of God. Services were held regularly morning and evening. Sunday School was well attended by young and old. The gospel was carried far and near by foot and by canoe. Medical work was done and many a poor and sick person benefited from this new care.

After a number of years of seemingly fruitless labour, in a fit of despondency Dugald Campbell called together the headmen of the district. He describes the day and night as dateless. There was no entry in his diary. It was a night when the sky was bestrewn with bright silver stars that shone and scintillated, and later on the smothered ember of a dying moon sank into the night behind the overshadowing hills. He sat in his homemade cottage by the Falls whose incessant roar pounded in his ear.

He told the men he was thinking of leaving the place to open up elsewhere among folk who would respond to his teaching. There had not been a single local conversion up to this time. In *Links of Help* (written later in 1916) he describes what happened.

"After long and loud discussion among themselves, Kasanga, a respected elder rose and spoke. 'White man and teacher,' he said, 'all you say is true, and we cannot deny a word. We appreciate all you have done for us, and are doing daily. We want to thank you on behalf of our brothers and sisters. But you don't know everything, white man. Listen. Do you know that when you came here, we had a camp near your mission station, the headquarters of a powerful secret society, where young people were herded promiscuously and taught wicked and abominable practices? But,' he continued, 'since you have come here, and as a result of your teaching the camp no longer exists and these practices have ceased. No,' he added, 'don't leave us, and when we understand your teaching we shall believe.'"

He could not say a word, and they separated. Next night he called them and said he would not leave them.

So he listened, and learned what he had not known about the silent and secret work of the Word of God in many hearts. From then on he saw a change. The hall was filled every Sunday. Many came daily to the morning and evening services. Attendances at school increased and confidence in the medical treatment grew. When they preached in the surrounding villages crowds gathered. Something was going on, something new. There was a movement afoot.

The movement broke out a few Sundays later. The hall was packed full, crowded to the door, and many stood to listen. Chiefs, people, government servants, soldiers and traders' employees all had packed into the place. Campbell had preached, and was almost through the service. A curious hush seemed to possess the people. There was a feeling that something was about to happen. It was apparent that the Holy Spirit was working. Between the last prayer and hymn there was a move in the congregation. All eyes were directed towards the intrusion, and some shrank back as a pock-faced man stood up and raised his head. He looked round the gathering, then at

Campbell, and spoke in a low, distinct, and clearly audible tone of voice. Here is what he said.

"Fathers, chiefs, headmen, and friends, and you, teacher, you all know me. I am Mitamba, the witchdoctor. My father was a witchdoctor before me, and it was from him that I learned the craft. He brought me up to the witch-burning business from the time I was a small boy. When I had learnt everything there was to learn, he gave me the 'hell-fetish'. Under his instruction I burnt my first witches, and did my first professional work. This morning I want to tell you all, and you, teacher, that I have been thinking over the Gospel and its claims for many months. I have slept little of late, and last night in despair I decided to accept Christ as my Saviour. I stand up to say that I am now a Christian. Look at me, friends. Watch me from now, and you will see I am a follower of Jesus - a Christian." He then sat down.

The effect of Mitamba's public confession could be described as electric. It was the first break in the Luapula. The following Sunday others came forward and made their own public confession of faith in Christ. So the effects of the work began to be seen and these continued week by week, and have continued till the present day. One of the happiest days in the life of Campbell at Johnston Falls was when he baptised the first group of believers. The baptism took place in the great river in the presence of a great crowd of people. This was at the very spot where they used to throw children to the crocodiles, where witch trials took place periodically, and where unabashed nude devil-dances were held.

As he immersed the converts, a monster crocodile rose to the surface only a few yards away and looked at the strange happenings with his fishy eyes, then slowly sank out of sight without interfering.

Many men and women, young and old, trusted the Saviour and went on to prove the reality of their faith. One of these was

Ina Chimbasule, a lady of over 100 years of age who said that as a girl she had known David Livingstone. She was baptised when she was over a hundred, a kindly old lady who regretted that her eyesight was so poor it prevented her from learning to read the Word of God. Because of her hearing difficulties she always sat on the front seat to be able to hear the preacher. She was an old worthy who would give some straight talk to the young women in their troubles and difficulties.

Imampundu was another Bantu granny who was a real helper and a trusty tribal adviser among women. Matters relating to birth, death and anything in between were always referred to her. She brought many to trust the Saviour.

Bwanika was another such lady. She used to visit distant villages and brought many women to the knowledge of salvation there. These were pioneering times and days of exploration. These believers formed the nucleus of a growing band whose number is now legion.

Among the other things that occupied Campbell's attention in these days was the translation of the New Testament into Bemba, the local language. He also translated and had printed a book of 200 hymns, the first contribution to hymnology in the local language. Eventually the National Bible Society of Scotland printed the four Gospels, the original copies of which can be seen to this day in Edinburgh. The whole Bible was completely translated at a later date.

CHAPTER 4

Deep Valley Experiences

Dugald Campbell records that his time at Johnston Falls was some of the finest years of his life. He was young, energetic and full of adventure. From this centre he went pioneering and trail-blazing. But these were also dark days. In this Luapula valley there are four graves which made it for him *THE VALLEY OF THE SHADOW*.

Half way between Livingstone's grave at Chitambo and Mambilima there is a small mound, crowned with a simple wooden cross. This was erected in memory of Helene, his little five year old daughter.

Toiling at Johnston Falls took its toll with the strain and anxiety of unavoidable hardships and privations. They were weakened by the daily menace of malaria despite daily doses of quinine, the consequent loss of appetite, low grade fever and anaemia. A trip to Luanza was considered. They boarded the mission boat and set off down the Luapula River to Lake Mweru and on to Luanza. There as a result of the anaemia and an irreducible temperature due to malaria Mrs Campbell gave premature birth to a son. They called him Ian. After only eleven days the mother died. What a sad day as they laid her body to rest in the cemetery up on the hill at Luanza overlooking Lake Mweru.

After his mother's death the baby was taken by two ladies who nursed and cared for him. Eventually Dugald Campbell with his two boys and the two ladies, Miss Merry and Miss Prentice, started the journey to Scotland. It was a journey full of hazards and trials. The baby became ill and eventually died of broncho-pneumonia at Mwenzo, Fife, on the Plateau. Thus there appeared another mound with a cross on top. One of the ladies took his remaining child to Scotland. The other lady returned to Luanza and later died at Johnston Falls.

Dugald Campbell FRGS

Campbell was stunned by this experience. He states that it took him nearly ten years to recover. At times like these one begins to ask why. The work had just got going. Temporary buildings had been erected. Classes had begun for many young people. They had baptised the first band of believers, and a few sick folk had been healed. Their notebooks were filled with language lore and vocabularies and they were looking forward to the dawn of a new day in the Luapula valley. But instead of dayspring arising and light breaking forth the darkness deepened. Johnston Falls, became a veritable Valley of the Shadow.

Dugald Campbell continued to labour for seven more years at Johnston Falls. Mr White from Australia came for a short spell. A B Patterson of London also gave help, and occasionally some others visited. But toil, travel and trial had taken their toll. Writing of these times he often pours out his heart, and one can feel his depression and despondency. He cannot speak calmly of the experience. He says it is the heart of darkness. Here is his description.

> "Men prowled about like wild animals and preyed on their fellows, clothed in skin of lion, leopard or crocodile. They cut each other with steel claws, ripped up, disembowelled, dismembered, tore to bits, and afterwards gorged and glutted themselves on the quivering flesh of men, women and children who had become the innocent objects of their cruelty and cannibal lust. The Devil was thus incarnate throughout the Congo and its tributaries, and Bantuland begat beasts in human form."

Many were killed by lions that roamed freely. The postman was eaten near his house, a part of his skull, his fez cap and scattered letters left behind. Campbell's cook was dragged out of his hut and taken and he himself was nearly taken. These and more were the circumstances in which he lived.

A Dutch missionary gave him a dog, he called him Richter. He was a brave fighter against whose fury and ferocity few were able to stand. He held up a hyena, and brought a leopard to bay till Campbell was able to shoot them, a reliable friend who saved the life of not a few.

Beyond these experiences and encounters was the daily lonely drudgery of life, surrounded by diseases such as malaria, diarrhoea, dysentery, and Blackwater Fever. There was too a recurrent readiness to discouragement or "getting down in the dumps" at some trifling trouble. Years and years of patient plodding, faithful teaching and hopeful preaching were passing. Long silent years of seemingly fruitless sowing of the seed made him doubtful of a harvest. But, at last! at last! it came. The dawn of a new era for the Gospel, and there broke into the Luapula valley simple Bible Christianity and all it stands for.

Here was a man of like passions such as we are, who knew the ups and downs of life. He had his mountain top experiences and well as those of the deep valley. His whole interest was in the people and their customs and culture. He lived with them, worked with them, ate their food and absorbed their way of life.

In 1905 Mr and Mrs Lammond joined him and occupied his three roomed house, while he went to the hill at Chipundu to start another itinerating work. Again the spectre of sickness came among them. Mrs Lammond this time became ill with Blackwater Fever and died. He described her as one of the pluckiest women God ever made, fearless and tearless. Faithfully she passed away after only a few brief, bright years of devoted service for her Lord in Bantuland.

After the death of Mrs Lammond, Mr Lammond went home to the UK. When he later returned to Johnston Falls, Dugald Campbell went back to Britain. He had been in Africa for eleven years and this was his first furlough. Here he remarried and returned to the Luapula, eventually commencing a new work at Lake Bangweulu where the Lord continued to bless his service.

CHAPTER 5

Mr Lammond's First Journey in Africa

William Lammond was born on 5th November 1876. He left school at the age of eleven and went to work as an engineering apprentice. At the age of twenty he was saved and gave his life to the Lord Jesus. Immediately he began to 'gossip' the gospel to everyone he met. He spent part of 1899 in Liverpool with Mr F S Arnot, preparing himself for missionary service to which he was commended from his home church in Glasgow.

Bound for Africa, Mr Lammond left Liverpool on March 17th 1900 in the steamship *Hickla* and arrived at Benguela on the west coast of Africa some weeks later. As they drew near to land, the *Empress National* sailed close by. The ship's engineer drew his attention to the crowded fore deck: "These," he said, "are slaves going to be sold in the port they had just left." He could not believe what he just heard, but the truth of the matter was confirmed to him later.

This was his first encounter with slaves, and there would be many more on his journey to the interior. Passing through a village one day, out of curiosity he glanced in through the open door of a hut. There was a man lying in the middle of the hut with each leg on either side of a centre pole, his feet thrust through a slave yoke with a pin driven into a log between his ankles. Another hut held two girls similarly bound. He had stumbled on a depot where slaves were waiting for collection and dispatch.

Later on he and Mr John Clarke (commended from Glasgow in 1899 to work in Congo) met a caravan of slaves with a mob of fully armed traders. They tried to converse with their leader who was boasting they had 2,000 slaves. What sheer hardship and misery it represented. Women were tied together like animals, thin and haggard, loaded and carrying babies and with other little ones at their feet. The men were loaded up with long forked sticks fastened to their necks and tied to each man in front. Their loads were rubber, ivory, honey, copper wire bangles, and salt. These were heart breaking experiences for a new comer to Africa. It made him sick at heart.

Having done business at Benguela and arranged carriers it was time to set off on the walk into the interior. The main party, led by Mr Charles Swan (commended to Congo from Sunderland in 1887) set out and instructions were given for him to wait behind and they would come for him later. Disobeying orders he set off during the night with two carriers! The air was full of fine flies, he said it was like fairyland and enchanting beyond words. Mr Swan was rightly annoyed with him for taking the risk, and he paid rather dearly for it in the long run. It laid the foundation for months of malaria which nearly finished his African course before it had really started. He was young and inexperienced.

The next stage of the journey was 300 miles to Chilonda. Being last to set off he went to say good bye and when he shook hands he was told he was burning up. A thermometer in his mouth read 103 degrees F. The journey of 50 to 60 miles was over mountains at 6,000 feet. Arriving at camp he threw himself down, ate and went to sleep, his temperature now 105 degrees.

From then on the journey was a nightmare. He was sick and miserable and a real burden to Mr Swan. "No man lives unto himself", and our careless actions can bring grief not only to ourselves but to others. His fevers continued for the next 3 to 4 months until he was down to skin and bone and weighed a mere 7 stones. However, a missionary doctor from America "happened" to be visiting. He had the latest treatment for malaria which set him on the road to complete recovery.

At Chilonda a caravan was waiting to take the party on to the interior. Being so ill his colleagues wanted him to return to the UK. But feeling God had called him to Africa he refused to listen. He was prepared if necessary to add to the considerable number of young fellows who had died before they had spent more than a couple of years in Africa. Mr and Mrs Dugald Campbell moved on with the caravan, and John Clarke waited with him.

The journey with John Clarke gave them time to learn something about the African people. On reaching Bihe in Angola they moved on into Lovale country. The first stretch of 500 miles was the most trying. It was the wet season and many hours and very many miles of wading through flooded plains were required. One stretch over the Cifumaje Flats involved five days of wading hour after hour, finding raised patches to camp on, the water seldom less than a foot deep. Sometimes it was up to their necks. It was on this stretch that they passed the caravan of slaves. How they made it through would remain a mystery.

The next excitement came when they were attacked by robbers. Because the party was strung out with about a mile between the head and the tail it was easy to be attacked. For a few days they walked more closely together, John and he bringing up the rear. But next their carriers revolted and went off leaving them with only two young boys. They sat down for a long wait until they could get other carriers. However the 'rebels' had sat down in the next valley and considered their situation. They had come 1000 miles and to return without completing their task would be a total loss for them. They returned and gave no more trouble.

On reaching Lovale land Mr Lammond spent the next three months with Mr and Mrs Fisher. In August the next lot of carriers arrived and they set off on the next stage of the journey. Having been on the journey for one year they were learning a fair amount of the language and had quite a good vocabulary. One day there was great hilarity when he shouted out at the top of his voice a certain word to ask for its meaning. It was rather a vulgar word!!

Eventually they reached the Lualaba river and set up camp. There were hippos downstream so he went hunting. John was successful in killing one, so they moved camp to be near the big supply of meat. Now began the huge task of cutting up and drying what could not be eaten. It is amazing what a crowd of Africans can eat when supplies are abundant!

It was prayer meeting night when the group reached Mwena. They received such a great welcome from Mr George. The African women ran to meet their men. This was a sight to see! Their bodies were "whitened" to show the gladness of their hearts. They threw themselves at their men folk, shouting and *hululuaing* as they welcomed them back from the 1,000 mile trip. The men had stopped at a river and had a good wash before decking themselves out in all the finery they had brought with them. What a reunion it was - most unusual for Africa!

A few days were spent in Mwena where they paid their respects to the Belgian officials. Mr George decided he was due a holiday and so he arranged to accompany them to Luanza another 200 miles further on. They arrived there in late September 1901, having left Liverpool on March 17th 1900. It had taken them eighteen long months to make the journey.

CHAPTER 6

Mr Lammond's Early Years

From his base at Luanza Mr Lammond made a number of visits to Johnston Falls in 1901, 1902 and 1903. In 1904 he married Flora Merry, his first wife. To do this he walked 250 miles to Abercorn (now Mbala in Zambia) at the lower end of Lake Tanganyika and then 250 miles back. On the return journey she nearly died of Blackwater Fever - a complication of severe malaria often associated with high quinine usage.

The Lammonds moved to Johnston Falls in August 1905 to meet a need and to assist Dugald Campbell. It is difficult for us now to realize that all the believers there were known by name. Very soon after his arrival at Johnston Falls the house he had built was burnt down by accident. These were difficult days.

In 1906 more and greater disaster struck again when Flora Lammond succumbed again to Blackwater Fever and died. The site for her burial was chosen with great care and her body laid to rest. Dugald Campbell and he then discussed which one should take a break first and return to the UK. They both were grieving over the loss of a wife. It was decided that Mr Lammond should go first. So with six carriers he set of on the 1,500 mile journey through Katanga to Luanda. He said only a "long walk" would help lift the sadness from his heart.

Boarding a steamer he returned to Britain. One of the first things he did was to attend a 12 month medical course at Livingstone College, London. This had been set up to train missionaries for emergency medical work and included anything from minor surgery to delivering babies.

In 1908 he married Miss Dora Gammon and she returned with him to Johnston Falls. They settled into the work and Mr Patterson, Mr Shapland and Mrs Lammond began to develop the school work. The power of the gospel was now being seen in those who trusted the Saviour. The absolutely devilish character of all native rites and ceremonies, the filthy lives of most of the people who came under the power of the gospel were changed. Sixty two men and women openly confessed to be following the Lord.

The school room was now not big enough for the children, and the church services are packed full. Children sit on the floor and there is no room to stand to sing. The condition of the air inside the hall is beyond description. A woman came from twenty miles away to hear the Word of God and openly confessed faith in Jesus Christ.

It became evident that they needed to build a new hall. The Christians were taught the principles of giving. The people brought what they could - little baskets of meal, beans and corn, or two or three eggs, and some managed to bring a penny. W L sighed and said, "I only wish I could borrow some of the empty halls at home!"

Mrs Lammond tells of a great work developing amongst the women as around 30 to 40 come to read the Word of God. She tells of how difficult it is to live as a Christian wife. In many cases she is one of many wives in the family and has to obey the head-wife as well as her husband. He can beat her at any time and do what he likes to her.

Some ladies dress really grand, wearing beads so heavy that they can hardly bear the weight. They wear very little cloth and some only a skin. Some decorate their heads while others shave it. They carry their babies on their backs and the wee mites look so comfortable.

Inshinbalushala was a very old lady of unknown age who remembered Livingstone and had talked with Stanley. She had been born a slave and three times as a slave had been taken right across the country. On being liberated she found her way home. There she heard the gospel from many and trusted the Lord and was brought from the slavery of sin into the liberty of Christ Jesus. Mrs Lammond well remembered the day she told her story, there was not a dry eye in the congregation! If she had been living in some nearby parts she would have been burnt as a witch as is the case with nearly all old women there. When she requested baptism they felt unwilling to baptise her as she was so frail, but accepted the will for the deed and received her into full church fellowship.

Mr A E Shapland tells of a time of great excitement in 1909. Mr Lyons, the magistrate of the district, was coming to visit the mission along with the big chief, Old Kazembe. One Saturday about 1pm the commotion was heard. Shapland had never seen anything like it. Drums beaten, bells ringing, flags flying, people shouting - what an uproar! Kazembe himself was carried in a hammock. Given a seat on the veranda, all the lesser chiefs from miles around surrounded Kazembe. Mr Lyons had a lot to say to the people.

Next morning saw the largest gospel meeting ever held at Johnston Falls. There were over 700 present, it was so big they had to gather under the trees. Chief Kazembe came with all his elders and at least twelve other chiefs. Shapland reports you could have heard a pin drop as Mr Campbell preached and told out the story of the Cross. This was a great opportunity and they trusted that many would respond to the Saviour.

During this year Dugald Campbell left Johnston Falls to commence a new work at Lake Benguela. Mr Patterson describes his farewell meeting. It was held outside on the veranda of Mr Lammond's house. Many believers told their testimony and declared their faith in Jesus Christ. Most had been brought to faith through the preaching of Mr Campbell. Their love for him was evident and many tears were shed as he left them.

Mrs Lammond gave an account of a trip that was made in the wet season later that year. She and W L started off for Ndola to collect loads of goods. Even today this is a daunting journey of at least 300 miles. There were no roads and they had to walk. So packing the tent, pots and pans, table and chairs, and a minimum of needed clothes, they set off. The first night they had thunder and lightening and torrential rain. Their tent was small and there was only one spot where they could pitch their tent. A lion let out a roar as it passed by. The mosquitoes never let up and often got into the tent.

Crossing rivers was most interesting. In the dug-out canoe they were so low in the water it felt like it was overturning. The crocs were all around and the boys were most anxious for their lives. Five times they had to make bridges. William felled a tree on each side of the river, they crashed against each other and thus made the start of a bridge. It was easy for the boys to sure footedly walk over with their loads, but for Mrs Lammond really difficult, especially with a fast flowing river underneath. She climbed from branch to branch, then onto one of the boy's shoulders - but into the river she went! William caught her and eventually they reached the other side wet but safe and well. She wrote, "Our good little boy had a cup of tea waiting for us in a nice little shady corner."

Mrs Lammond went on to tell that it had been a difficult year because of so much rain, and observes that this happens every third year. Food supply is difficult and the people are starving. William went to get them meat. "He is not a good shot," she said, and cartridges were few. So they made it a matter of prayer that he would have good success and plenty of meat with few shots. With what joy they returned to the village. The zebras were very tender, and she boiled the tongues and ate them for supper! The meat was then dried over a fire - it keeps for weeks but smells terrible! All were now well fed.

The work went on steadily, and there were many stories of conversions and baptisms. But the problem of Sleeping Sickness continued and the people have all been withdrawn from the riverbank. School work was going forward - the boys are good at reading but writing is poor. Amongst the girls it is less encouraging - they get married, lose interest in reading and spend their days in routine work and gossip. Each Friday is given over to Bible stories and they remember these stories very well.

Mr Lammond gave a detailed account of the meetings held each week. Each morning there were prayers Monday – Friday at 6am, and school each afternoon. Tuesday evening was Bible reading. Wednesday the men and women met separately - there were many babies at the women's meeting. Thursday was for believers and on Friday the lads came from the villages for teaching. Saturday was the prayer meeting. The Sunday service started with gospel preaching at 8am, this was followed by the Breaking of Bread (Communion). After lunch they visited surrounding villages with the gospel and returned late in the evening, rather tired.

Mr Shapland tells of many open doors, and visiting villages as far as 40 miles distant. Speaking with an old man he asked him how he understood the message. "Yes," he said, "the words are good and true, but how are we to know and understand? We have no teacher and this is only the third time in five years we have heard the message."

Mr Patterson tells of the continuing expansion of schools in another two villages. The Christians have given a month's free labour towards the building of the school rooms.

The school room at Johnston Falls is coming on nicely - the building holds 500 with an extra five small classrooms. There are no seats so the children will sit on the floor. With the little money they have they will pay the teachers themselves and look to the Lord for His help. A teacher's wage was thirty shillings a month (£1.50 in today's currency).

Mr Lammond gave more details of how they built their hall. They had little money and the weekly collection was very small. Some of the men brought a few pence - the average wage is five shillings a month (or 25 pence per month today). The women brought little baskets of meal, beans, rice and eggs. This was all put aside for the building. They prayed long and hard during the rainy season and all the church joined in. The answer came from the inside in an unexpected way. All who had taken on the Name of the Lord would give one month of free labour and service.

The women carried water half a mile from the river and the men made bricks. Those unable to come got someone to take their place and they had a full muster. Work started on the 23rd June 1909 with prayer and praise. One of the older women took charge as overseer. Over the month they carried water every day - even the slower ladies would walk the equivalent of 10 miles per day with water. They kept at it even though some of the older ones were tottering, but they did it heartily "as unto the Lord".

Mr Patterson and Mr Shapland worked hard and in just under three months the hall was complete, debt free. Seats were supplied later.

Sadly on the morning of opening the building the government doctor examined for signs of Sleeping Sickness. One man has fallen sick! Will this spread?

Mr Lammond was finding that the medical training received at Livingstone College was being used more and more. A number of Europeans as well as local folks were coming for help. A man who was involved in a shooting accident was brought for help. The leg was in such a bad condition that the only answer was to amputate. The description of the conditions for the surgery was not recorded, only to say they were unfavourable. The operation was a success and the leg healed nicely. His next job was to make an artificial leg.

Mrs Lammond's health was much improved and she was able to take up work again after a long illness. Hospital and school work expanded at this time. Miss Coponet was giving good service in the hospital in the mornings, and at the school in the afternoons. Dispensary work was becoming more and more important too in these days. Most days 20 to 30 patients were being seen.

Then the dreaded Sleeping Sickness struck. The whole population of Johnston Falls was evacuated and moved 45 miles away to Kaleba, a place away from the river and much more healthy. There was great hardship amongst the people. They had little in the way of physical reserve and many died of starvation. No transport was available and all their belongings had to be carried on their heads. Poverty was intense and there was nowhere to live. They had to make their own shelters from what they could find.

This chapter in the history of what was to become Mambilima closes rather sadly.

CHAPTER 7

The Kaleba Years

Kaleba, the place to which they all had to go is an area 45 miles north of Johnston Falls on the road to Mbereshi, Kazembe and Lake Mweru. It lies a little farther away from the Luapula River and therefore there is less danger from the tse-tse fly. But there was a problem of a severe shortage of food, and it is recorded they had to travel up to 40 miles to get a very little. As a result there was much sickness and many died. Also a leopard stalking the area gave great concern before they were able to kill it.

There were very few young men in the village as they had now begun to drain away to work in the expanding copper mines on the Copperbelt. This can change men's attitude to life, and when they returned they were so arrogant. They now treated the message of the gospel with contempt.

Mr Lammond gave much help to the people in building their simple houses. All the houses are of the same style - a square box made with sun dried mud bricks, divided into four small rooms by cross shaped walls with openings to allow access into all the rooms. A piece of cloth or sacking hangs in the openings for a door. The walls do not rise fully to roof height, so air, smells and sounds flow freely within the house. Tree saplings are cut in the forest and tied together with bark string to make the frame of a peaked roof. Grass is then cut in the bush and laid as thatch for the outside roof. The floor consists of compacted mud into which some naturally occurring coloured dust is added to give it a colourful finish. This requires a bit of effort but it is very cost effective!

All the houses lined the roadside, which made it much easier for visitation using their bicycles. The magistrate and Medical Officer were to be congratulated on moving around 12,000 people safely to this area.

The old were treated very harshly, especially the women. In the temporary hospital was one such lady who was found lying at the roadside exhausted. She had been chased out of the village and beaten with sticks by the children who were encouraged to do this. Her only crime was that she was old and useless at a time when food was scarce. It was great to see the change when the gospel of Jesus Christ arrived - dignity of life is brought to all age groups. Miss Nisbet was with them, caring for those who were sick. They had some lymph and she vaccinated all that came her way, and went out to the villages to treat those who were in need. There were also many lepers in this area. Miss Nisbet had the joy of telling them of the Saviour and a good number trusted Him for salvation.

When the first baptisms took place at Kaleba it was a time of great rejoicing. There were three men and seven women. Buleni (this means *to give*) was a young man about 20 years old. He said, "I once heard Mr Campbell teaching 'He that believeth on the Son hath everlasting life, but he that believeth not the Son shall not see life but the wrath of God abideth on him'." The message gripped him and he was led to see that the only way of salvation was by trusting the Lord Jesus.

Pandawe, a young man of about the same age, spoke thus: "For several months I was sick and vomiting blood. I was very sick indeed, and then I read in the gospel of Mark chapter 5, verse 25, of a woman who had an issue of blood twelve years who was healed by touching Jesus. I could not forget this, and I thought if the Lord could do this for a woman who was sick for twelve years, He could do it for me. Thus I came to Jesus." Teaching people to read is of great value.

The third man Kanenene (meaning *little ant*) had been a slave in Mushidi's capital. When the Belgians killed Mushidi all the slaves were set free, and Kanenene returned to the Luapula. He gave his testimony of being a witchdoctor who was called here and there to treat sick people. Then his own child of five years old was very ill, and he was going to prepare some of his evil mixtures to treat him. The child pleaded, "Father, don't do it!" He was challenged by this and thought to himself how he had been deceiving people with his 'medicines' all these years. So he rejected them and obeyed God and trusted in Jesus Christ.

There were two very earnest women at Kaleba. The first was Incapasa (meaning *mother of twins*) and the other Tintulwilwa. The former related well to scores of women in neighbouring villages, and was keen on attending marriages and funerals, thus witnessing for the Lord quietly but effectively over a large area.

At Salanga (a village about seven miles north) there was a group of people who were expressing a desire to follow "the way". This is how they put it: *Ku konka nshila iyi. Nshila* is the word for a single file path, a native path, not the made-up road of the European - that is "*musebo*" and is equivalent to the broad way. These were the first to follow the Lord Jesus in this village.

School work was bringing great blessing. The teachers saw many trusting the Lord. The faith of many was feeble and they needed much teaching of the Word. A picture of the Christians taken here in 1915 shows 90 people in the photo.

Mr Lammond continued his wide interests and undertook a great variety of work. In 1915 he writes of translating the book of Psalms but was having great difficulty getting the correct sense. He also made a collection of about 400 native songs connected with various interests of life. He kept up the gruelling pace of teaching the scriptures in at least two villages each day. He had to walk from village to village and get back home before dark. There were now 23 lads teaching in eight schools, with their pay varying from 2s. 6d. to 6s. 6d. per month (equals 12p to 30p today). He said he was trying to impress upon the church the privilege of helping by giving, but up to the present they did not see it that way. The weekly collection was very small, only 6d. to 9d.

These schools were very primitive, just a fence of grass 6 feet high around a big tree. A few poles laid across short forked sticks made seats for a mass of wriggling chocolate-brown, youthful humanity, up to all the tricks of their more civilised contemporaries, and with a few of their own special invention; for example, getting a grasshopper to jump on the back of a 'swotter' who is bravely trying to print a capital K with a grubby forefinger on the carefully levelled ground. They were doing well after only a fortnight. Many could repeat verses of scripture and when it came to singing they just let themselves go. Sometimes it was difficult to recognise the tune but the harmony was great.

These were difficult years at Kaleba with much poverty, disease and sickness. There was a bad flu epidemic and many died, and likewise a bad outbreak of measles left many of the children blind. Two of the believers' children were left in this condition. WL cried out to God for a doctor. Oh for a man or woman with the love of God in their heart and the skill that can only come with proper training to serve in this area.

During these years Mr and Mrs Lammond returned to

England for a furlough. While there, World War I commenced and they found themselves stranded in the UK. However WL did not waste his time. His wife's cousin, Ernest Scott, was a dental practitioner in Bournemouth and Willie went to stay with him. He proved himself to be an apt pupil. When this cousin went on holiday a year later Willie Lammond took over the practice! Before returning to Zambia, he had registered as a dentist in Britain.

His knowledge of dentistry proved to be a great benefit to the Africans. People often travelled hundreds of miles for treatment. On one occasion, a huge African who needed a back tooth extracted got to the stage of allowing WL to fix his forceps in position. But then the big man took fright and refused to let him proceed. "Then take it out yourself, you big baby," said WL and walked away. The fellow did not have much choice. The forceps were clamped firmly on the offending molar. He wrenched the instrument from his mouth and made one of the neatest extractions ever seen!

While in Scotland Mr Lammond met many interested people who would help the work forward. One of these he records as Mr Robert Sharp of Cowdenbeath. As a very young boy I can just remember this man. He and his brother had a draper's business in the town, and personally I am most interested to discover this link with my home town.

Recently a nephew of Mr Sharp told me how his uncle had visited Mr Lammond at Mambilima, and later Mr Lammond recalled to him that during the visit Mr Sharp had been preaching about the Tabernacle. But it became so difficult for Mr Lammond to translate the message that he abandoned translating and just gave a message of his own!

Another one he met was Mr Fred Elliott, an evangelist. He and Mr Sharp became interested in mission work. Miss Betty

Fraser who came out to Johnston Falls as a nurse in 1925 was converted at one of Mr Elliott's meetings.

Invited to a tent to hear Mr Fred Elliot preaching the gospel, she discovered that all she had been depending on for eternity swept from under her feet. She trusted the Lord Jesus as her Saviour. About a year later she attended a missionary meeting at which Mr G H Mowat of Angola was speaking. Arriving late she slipped into the gallery and sat in the dark. She had just sat down when Mr Mowat put a picture on the screen of a nurse at his station who had just died. He said, "I believe that God is going to call somebody in this meeting to take her place." Miss Fraser immediately said to herself, "Here I am Lord, send me!" and from that day she prepared herself for the mission field.

The day before the Lammonds left Glasgow a bright capable young man by the name of Mr C E Stokes asked to speak to Mr Lammond. "Would I be a suitable person to join the work in the schools at Johnston Falls," he asked. Mr Lammond was shocked as he did not think this man was so interested. But Mr Stokes prepared himself and came out. Someone said to Lammond, "That is the biggest fish that has been caught in Glasgow!" WL replied, "I did not catch him, he jumped into the boat!" It was the Lord's doing and when Mr Stokes arrived in 1926 the work took on a completely different character.

During the Lammonds' absence the work had continued well and many had come to the Lord for salvation. The school work progressed, with 22 students in the advanced class each morning, and the basic school in the afternoon had over 100 pupils.

It was during these years that the first Luapula conference was held. It was 1920, when several missionaries from the area gathered to have a time of fellowship. Included in this number were Mr and Mrs Dan Crawford.

Then in 1922 the news was received with great joy that that the ban had been lifted on the Luapula and the people were free to return to Johnston Falls. So started the long trek back on foot, once again carrying their many goods and chattels with them.

CONFERENCE GROUP, KALEBA.

Back Row—Miss Elliot, Mrs. Higgins, Mrs. Turner (L.M.S.), Mrs. Anton.
Second Row—Mr. Higgins, Mr. Crawford, Mrs. W. Lammond, Mrs. G. W. Sims, Mrs. Crawford (with Gwen Sims), Mr. Anton.
Third Row—Mr. M'Kenzie, Mr. W. Lammond, Mrs. Last.
Front Row—Mr. Ellis, Tommy Higgins, Mr. G. W. Sims, Mr. Last.

Footnote:
This picture was taken by Mr Robert Sharp referred to on p 49 during his visit to Africa. He supplied several such pictures in *Dan Crawford of Luanza* by James J Ellis (John Ritchie Ltd, Kilmarnock).

CHAPTER 8

Return to Johnston Falls (1922-26)

On returning from Kaleba, work began on the same site they had left twelve years before. The first tasks were to make houses that were habitable again. They then commenced to build a hall as a meeting place for the church.

This hall was quite a building. The main supporting pillars consisted of huge trees which had been cut down in the forest and manhandled into position. There was great rejoicing when they were erected in position and the task accomplished without injury.

The new hall was opened in October 1923 amid great rejoicing. Over 1,162 people were present plus over 100 infants. It took a lot of packing to get them all inside and the children made it rather noisy. Mr Anton, Mr Sims, Mr G Lammond and Mr W Lammond took part. This was followed by a Communion Service attended by 700, although only 200 broke bread. The appropriate reverence and godly order were very marked.

The collection was a record £2. 7s. 4d (approx £2.35 at present) - most of it was mites valued at around one fortieth of a penny each. The corner of the hall was given over to the collection 'in kind' - little and big baskets, basins and bowls of maize, meal, millet, eggs, etc. How they had managed to carry eggs in their pockets without crushing them was a mystery. It was a time of great rejoicing.

Mr and Mrs George Lammond were going on leave and Mr J F McKenzie from Australia came to take over the work in their absence. He had the great joy of seeing the work expand further. Regularly people were giving their lives to Jesus Christ and publicly confessing this by being baptised in the river.

A witchdoctor turned to Christ and sent his basket of fetishes to be burnt. An old headman from the village had a dream. In it he dreamt he had died. When he awoke he repented and trusted the Lord and put away all his witchcraft medicines.

Mr and Mrs Willie Lammond returned again from leave in 1925. They were accompanied by Miss Beatrice (Betty) Fraser from Aberdeen. As a registered nurse she was to be a great asset to the medical work which now began to be better organised. She moved forward and set up a small dispensary. Now a number of people were being treated as in-patients. A lady with "dropsy" had fluid drained from her legs, and a boy who had been mauled by a crocodile was treated successfully. Both of these people gave themselves to the Lord Jesus Christ.

The year 1926 was to be a most eventful year. There were floods in the valley such as they had never seen before. The Luapula River rose an extra 45 feet and flooded the whole village. It was the growing season and the gardens were ruined with no hope of vegetables for a long time. It caused great hardship in the village and travel was impossible.

Preparations were made for a conference to be held at Johnston Falls in the month of July. Dan Crawford had been asked to come as a speaker, but news came by a fast cycle rider that Dan Crawford had died. He had passed into the presence of his Lord on 3rd June. As the news of his death spread, many from the village gathered at the hall. By 3.30pm the hall was full to overflowing. Mr Crawford's position in the country was unique. The older generation looked up to him as their *"Mukulu"* meaning 'aged one', respected and esteemed. We translate this approximately as 'elder'.

It was a very emotional gathering and it was difficult to keep back tears. Memories were stirred, for it was Crawford who came with Pomeroy and had encouraged Mr Lammond to come in 1905. In the company were many who remembered his coming. Mr Crawford had found a people plunged in heathen darkness, idolatry, spirit worship and even cannibalism. Secret societies with gruesome rites wielded power over the people. Satan received homage from his worshippers as "Chief of the Spirits". Witchcraft and witch burning were the rule, with mutilation and cruel punishment meted out to defaulters. Nowhere was the name of Jesus even known.

Here were the sons and daughters of these same people, a big crowd of them, met in quiet, subdued sorrow to record their debt to the one who had passed away. There was a deep note of praise that Dan Crawford had lived to see these terrible things give place to the gospel, to a decent government, and to a measure of civilisation. He left behind him several thousand believers in the Lord Jesus Christ who were mourning the passing of their "Elder".

In rapt attention and with a hush hanging over the congregation appeals were made not to let slip the precious blessing which under God, *Konga Vantu* had brought to the district (this was his native name meaning *Gatherer of the People*). Some remembered his own words, "Africa shall have my bones".

His translation of the New Testament was in use, and the Old Testament was ready for the press. The financial help he had given was enormous. In the district hundreds were able to read the New Testament because of the generous help the school work had received from him.

Much praise was given to God and many prayers were offered

for Mrs Crawford that God would support her in her grief. Their only surviving son was in Scotland.

Two days after that sad meeting a letter was received from Luanza saying that Dan Crawford hoped to be with them at the conference on the 24th July. But the sad news of his going home to heaven had arrived before the letter.

The conference went ahead, and there was a great spirit of oneness in the gatherings. The numbers were very large and the native brethren and sisters had their ideas on hospitality expanded. The open air meetings in the moonlight were an inspiration.

W L said it was worth all the years in Africa to see this, and to think he had actually arrived in the valley when there was not a single believer in it. His regret was the Mr Crawford had not lived to see such a gathering. The quiet hush at the Communion Service made them feel and know the Lord's presence among them. In the congregation was a dear old tottering man who had been a soldier in Mushidi's evil army. Now he was saved and a new man in Christ.

At the conference Mr Anton dealt with many subjects including the scope of the responsibilities of believers such as the following:

1. Individual responsibilities of native Christians.
2. Responsibilities in households; better home conditions to guard against sin.
3. Responsibility to the community; be industrious, obey government ordinances, respect those in authority.
4. Responsibility of the church to preach the gospel; Christians to undertake financial responsibility towards the Lord's work.

Mr Lammond introduced the subject of attitudes to school and industrial work. He outlined a scheme which had a central school for teachers, thus enabling them to comply with government regulations, and would train native leaders for the work. The Bible would be the authority for all moral conduct and religious teaching. Education would also be given to promising boys and girls in both mental and manual work. School work and industrial work would be taught side by side. Boarding schools would be preferable to day schools.

1926 was the year that Mr C E Stokes joined the work. He was a school master and it would be him who would put school work on a proper footing. It was envisaged that he would organise and run the whole educational programme.

This was also the year when Miss Ethel Woolnough came. For the first time the girls too had a trained teacher. It was gratifying to see such progress in both the medical and the educational fields.

Johnston Falls Church Meeting Room, 1929

CHAPTER 9

More about Mr Lammond

1. Animal Adventures

Mr Lammond never claimed to be the best shot in the world with a gun, but many times it saved his life. He first learned to handle a gun as a youth of 21 when he joined the 6th Battalion Highland Light Infantry Volunteers in Glasgow. One day the officer in charge found him standing idly with the butt of his rifle on the ground and one hand over the muzzle. He stopped in front of him, and in full view of everyone he opened up a volley from all his guns on him. In strong language he shouted, "What kind of a —— fool are you to have a rifle?" - and on and on he went. Snapping to attention, Lammond kept his mouth shut and took it on the chin. He was left feeling the size of nothing, much to enjoyment of his friends.

But this taught W L a lesson which possibly saved his life. In 1906 while hunting for buck he stood underneath a tree which his helper had climbed to try to spot the game. He automatically took up a "stand in case" attitude, his rifle loaded. Unknown to him a blade of grass had got across the trigger and as he lifted it to his shoulder the gun went off. The blast hit his face, the bullet whizzed past his nose only inches away. He could not tell whether his head was still intact or not. When he realized he was still in one piece he gave thanks for the captain who taught him a vital lesson nine years earlier.

Camping in the bush with a colleague and a few carriers they were worried one night by the sound of two lions prowling around. It was dark and the lions were too near for comfort, they were tightening their circle round the camp. His friend had a pistol which he thought might frighten the beasts. He pointed the revolver in the direction of the sound and fired. The growling stopped, nothing more was heard. In the morning they checked the area around them and there was one dead lion. It had been dragged a distance by the other lion, but there was no sign of a wound. On examination they found that the bullet had penetrated the eye and entered the brain. Now who had guided that shot? Was it just coincidence? Or was it the evidence of a much Higher Hand?

On another bush trip he was with two government officials. Before supper, some mail had arrived including a large parcel. It contained a "bulala" lamp. This is a hunting lamp that fits on the forehead with a battery strapped on the shoulder. They tried it to see that it was working. The owner picked up his rifle to test the sighting. To his amazement he found himself looking into two amber eyes nearby. Carefully taking aim he fired and the eyes disappeared. Everyone went to sleep. In the morning they found a full grown lion dead with a bullet between the eyes. Was this another coincidence or another example of that protection by the Higher Hand?

Another night he was staying in Mukwampas' village. In the early hours of the morning he was wakened by screaming and shouting from the other side of the village. Soon it stopped and he went off to sleep again. Shortly after daybreak a man and his wife came to his tent. The man had his scalp badly torn, in fact almost torn off. The story was that during the night a lion had come to their door. Hearing the noise the man went to the door and opened it a little. The lion grabbed him, sinking its claws into his skull and tried to drag him out of the hut. A great struggle took place, his wife sprang to his help along with much shouting and screaming.

Eventually the scalp tore, the man fell back into the hut and his wife quickly shut the door. The scalp was in a bad way and the skull too was scratched. W L cleaned it, disinfected it and stitched the wound as carefully as he could, trusting and praying that it would heal. Returning a few weeks later he found it had in fact completely healed. Mr Lammond remarked that if the casualty had been a European he most probably would have died.

Tales of encounters with lions go on and on. Old Charlie was a well known lion who had killed many a person in his area. He entered a village but came off second best to an old lady. The door of her hut was just reeds. He tried to force his way into this hut but got stuck fast in the doorway. After getting over her fear and shock she started throwing her pots at Charlie's head, clay pots which one by one smashed over his head. The old woman screamed and screamed but no one answered. In desperation she took a live firebrand and pushed it into Charlie's face. With a great roar he pulled himself free and backed off making loud, wild noises. The place was like a battlefield, broken pots everywhere, the hut badly damaged but the old lady triumphant! She was the only one whom Charlie attacked and lived to tell the tale!

Snakes are always a great danger and are very common in these parts. Some are harmless but many are really deadly – it is difficult to tell at a glance which is which. So the principle to observe is that the only safe snake about the place is a dead one. Snakes mostly attack humans in self-defence. If a person makes the attack accidentally or deliberately the snake's reaction is quick - it rears up and strikes or spits according to its character.

The worst experience that W L had was with a spitting snake. He met it on the path he was walking on and hit it with his walking stick. But the blow was not fatal. It reared up and for a split second he saw its mouth open and he looked down its throat. He struck it again and killed it but at the same moment it spat at him and the venom landed in his eyes. Instantly he was blinded and in great pain. Little could be done.

He lay down and got one of his carriers to pour water from his water bottle into his eyes. More water was brought and they kept pouring it into the eyes. Eventually they brought his travelling trunk. His boy opened it and brought out the accident case. In it was a syringe and ophthalmic tablets but no one could read the labels. Exasperated, he ordered the boy to read the letters: a-t-r-o- ... No! No! not that one! Then c-o-c- ... Yes! that one! He put a tablet in each eye and the pain subsided. He was blind so the boy led him to the next village. They laid him out on a stretcher in a dark hut, put a handkerchief soaked in water over his eyes and he went to sleep. When he awoke his eyes were weak but he could see. Next day he was fine, he washed out his eyes with permanganate and went on his way!

The Luapula River in these days was full of hippos. One day they were escorting Mrs Crawford on her way to Luanza in the metal boat when the cry went up that there was a hippo nearby. The mighty beast saw them and came at them. It hit the boat broadside on with such a force it dented the boat. The hippo then left the river and climbed the bank. They went after the huge animal but soon discovered that there were two of them. Taking aim they shot the first one and it rolled over. Suddenly they were being attacked by the second hippo. It nimbly jumped over the first one and came at them. They cried, "Back! Back!" and tried to run off. This was almost impossible, and in desperation they lifted Grace Crawford and threw her up into a tree. Eventually they were able to deal with the other hippo and kill it too.

W L did not know which tree Grace was in, and was retuning to the boat to show her the hippos. Passing under the tree he heard the voice calling, "Mr Lammond!" There she was, stuck in this large thorn bush. Jumping down her clothing was so badly torn that W L laughed out loudly at the state she was in. She replied, "Take a look at yourself!" His shirt was in threads too. They all laughed at each other so much, but it was with joy and rejoicing that they were safe. It was great fun to see those normally staid and stylish Europeans in tatters!

2. The Teaching of Crafts and Skills

At a conference for missionaries on the subject of teaching practical skills, Mr Lammond was asked to present a paper on "Industrial Training". This was a subject he did not like in case it conveyed the impression that "an industry" was being used to support mission work, and with it would come the great temptation to make it a paying concern, to make it pay at all cost, with negative results. W L preferred to teach crafts and skills in such a way that people would be enabled to improve their own standard of living, to make things and do things for themselves, thus improving family living conditions and overcoming local handicaps.

In most parts of Central Africa the ordinary African suffers from many severe handicaps. First the food is not sufficiently good and lacks variety, so that most of them are undernourished and many children and adults die from malnutrition. There are also very poor standards of hygiene. Every craft and skill acquired would be an added weapon with which to fight these handicaps.

W L went on to describe how education was changing beyond the teaching the basic "three Rs" to try to fit the people to be better Christians, better parents and better citizens. He said, "Nowadays times are changing, and the government is imposing restrictions on how missions operate. Conditions are laid down that involve significant changes all round. The rising generation are keen to do things for themselves, and there is a need for 'book learning'".

This 'teaching and doing' was the obvious way forward for W L. He reckoned that as most missionaries had come to preach the gospel they were not really prepared to teach skills. Although most missionaries do impart to others a skill of some sort, a planned and organized approach would be more beneficial.

All the people in the area were peasant farmers, so he thought the first line of approach should be in agriculture. The area is fertile and more could be done in the cultivation of vegetables, maize and oil palms. There was a need to introduce and grow new and better varieties which are suitable for the country.

Looking back on this proposal after 50 or 60 years, little has changed. The cultivation methods and the variety of things grown are much the same. Have we let the African people down in this matter over these years?

Printing has been developed in some areas but this is limited. Tailoring has been introduced and one mission has introduced wickerwork. Pottery could be tried at small cost and outlay, for the clay is of good quality and plentiful.

At another conference of missionaries Mr Lammond made the suggestion for a team of practical workers who could go from station to station doing building and repair work. The idea was not taken up as they appeared to have enough work to do already. A chance remark heard later was to the effect that "the man who sees the need is probably the man called to the task". This led to the establishment in a small way of such a centre in Johnston Falls.

A number of lads were taught the elements of making and burning bricks, building, carpentry, furniture making, and wood turning. Others were taught how to repair shoes using good quality leather, also to repair cycles including brazing of frames. Iron work and soldering were also taught, and how to dye fibres and weave mats made of cord. This meant that other mission stations could be supplied with many essential items. Several of these lads did go to other areas where they used their skills for the benefit of these communities.

However, some missionaries look on such training as a waste of time and resources, because when trained, the person moves on to another area. W L advocated that a missionary must look on his work in an altogether different way. Let him think of it as a school or college where for a time individuals are under his care and tuition; then they move into the stream of life and do their work alongside their fellows. If sound Christian character building has been included in their teaching time, the teacher need not be over anxious about the final results - they can be left with God.

W L advised categorically:
"When teaching, insist on work being well finished. Show evidence of good sound workmanship and let the work have some character. Do not take short-cuts, they do not pay in the long run. Use what you find around you.

"Goods must be of best quality, or even fellow missionaries will object to paying for repairs that are sub standard. Be as much a missionary in your workshop as in the assembly. Remember the example of Him who said that He 'came not to be ministered unto, but to minister'."

3. Mr Lammond's House
Mr Lammond's House was built state of the art when he returned from Kaleba soon after 1922. It was built on a really beautiful site overlooking the Luapula River with a panoramic view of the rapids called Mambilima Falls. On the other side of the river lay Belgian Congo.

It was a grand two storey house with a large bay window on the ground floor. To the front there was a large veranda with a series of semi-circular steps leading down to a lined walkway to the river. In the centre of this walkway a sundial gave an accurate reading of the time of day. Unfortunately this has been stolen long ago!

The ground floor walls were built with large sun-dried mud bricks and were very thick, built in place with mud plaster. The floors were made of polished mud. The living room took up most of the ground floor and was a most spectacular area with its large bay window and plenty of room to entertain the many visitors who came. The other rooms downstairs were a kitchen and a bathroom - with a flushing toilet.

The bedrooms were upstairs. The reason for upstairs was the fear of wild animals such as lions. This was very real at the time as many such animals were in the vicinity, including a herd of elephants which could be destructive and dangerous. The upper floor was supported on wooden beams made from *mukwa* (mahogany) and the upper walls were of mud and wattle. The original roof was covered with grass thatch, but this was replaced with metal in 1961 because at that time arsonists posed a great danger.

Much more recently, Mr Kabwesha, the School Board Secretary, used to sleep on the living room floor when he visited the area. He usually slept in the same spot each time, but one night he chose to sleep at the bay window. During the night he was wakened by a thunderous roar. The ceiling had fallen in, right at the spot where he usually slept. He gave much thanks to God for His protection!

In 2003 the house had to be demolished because of its dangerous condition. The beams of the first floor were 20 cm x 20 cm and approx 7 metres long. They were solid *mukwa* and still in beautiful condition, as good as new. Wood cutters sawed these by hand to make planks 20 cm x 2.5 cm and 5 cm x 5 cm. This wood was used (recycled!) in the construction of the new school building.

A new three room bungalow has now been built on the site, and today is occupied by the head teacher of the High School and his family. The plumbing uses the original septic tank which has never required alteration or attention from the first day it was built, such was the high standard of its construction. And now there is no fear of wild animals, just an occasional snake poses some danger.

In 2004 Margaret and I were visited by the Detective Inspector of Police looking very worried. "There has been a theft from the Mission," he said with gravity. We were not aware of anything going missing. Reluctantly, we took him in our vehicle to see the prized "exhibit" as he kept calling it. Leaving us in the vehicle he disappeared into the village along with a shop owner to retrieve the "exhibit".

Thirty minutes later we see him coming towards us with two men running after him carrying a broken toilet pan with 6 feet of piping still attached. It had been taken from the site where Mr Lammond's house once stood. Protocol said we now had to take "it" to Police Headquarters. The Chief almost exploded when this "thing" was dumped in his office. "Take that outside," he said, "who would want such a smelly thing in his office?"

We laughed all the way home!

Mr Lammond's house with grass roof, 1930

Mr Lammond's house with tin roof, 1960

Mr Lammond's house being demolished, 2005

New house on site, 2007

CHAPTER 10

Developments in the 1930s

At the end of chapter 8 we noted the first arrivals of professionals in the nursing and educational fields. This enabled a great step forward to be made in both of these areas. Mr Stokes was leading the educational work. A school to teach teachers was begun and 80 candidates were enrolled. The vision was that on completion these teachers would go out to the villages and start school work there. Looking back one wonders how much this could have achieved? But in a situation where there was very little or nothing it was a big step forward.

The basic school commenced with 210 pupils. The facilities were very limited with virtually no equipment. Many times writing was done in the flattened smooth earth, then progressed to using slates, and eventually chalk, paper and pencil. The children were taught the basics of reading and writing. The New Testament now available in the local language was used as the text book.

Miss Woolnough was responsible for teaching the girls and women. She was happy to see 50 girls with New Testaments and able to read them. This was a tremendous advance to have women and girls being educated.

Mr Lammond included in the programme the teaching of skills and crafts. He had the ability to turn his hand to anything and so brick making and building was taught, also carpentry and turning skills. Thus a varied educational programme was established.

The medical work was developing under the leadership of Miss Fraser. At least a hundred patients were being treated each day at the dispensary, with dressings, injections and treatments being administered in very limited facilities.

During these years many building projects were undertaken on the mission. Mr Lammond would draw the plans for these, and his ideas were not to be questioned.

A school building with a central hall and two classrooms at either end was built. There was also office space and adjoining toilet facilities. The commemoration stone of the building was laid by Mr Swan in 1931 when he was visiting the mission. Mr Stokes described this as the best thing that Mr Lammond had done!

Johnston Falls School, original building, 1929

Johnston Falls School, "new" building, 1931

During these days the Scriptures were being taught and it was Mr Lammond's aim to have a Sunday School in every village and eventually a church established in each. The Word of God was preached, and young and old responded to the message and placed their faith in the Lord Jesus Christ. This was followed by their public confession of their faith by being baptised in the river. Mr Stokes told of 24 believers being baptised on Christmas Day one year, and this was repeated on a regular basis. Those baptised included a witchdoctor and a large number of chiefs.

Miss Woolnough too was glad to see many of the girls at the school trust the Saviour, and Mr Stokes reported that every boy in the boarding school had believed. These were most encouraging times.

The hospital work also led to many trusting the Lord Jesus. A Bible message was given to the people each day and regular personal visitation brought comfort to many. Month by month the numbers being treated increased. Miss Fraser's workload was getting greater, but she found the new hospital building very convenient for the work.

Mr Paterson came in 1931 and was a great help in the new senior school. Unfortunately he was killed while out elephant hunting. Mr Barham also arrived and remained in the work for two years.

In 1932 Chief Mulundu died. He had heard the gospel message often but would not respond to it. Many times he had discussed with the missionaries the matter of his 'latter end' but he did not believe. Everyone wondered why, being so interested, he would not yield to Jesus Christ. Eventually when he was at death's door the reason was discovered. It was his chief's "regalia" or special carb or insignia which was supposed to be supernatural and had to be worshipped at certain times.

Before he died he called Mr Lammond to his palace. In his

presence he named his son as his successor and said, "Let him take full control, I hand it to him. Now for me there is nothing left to do now except to take Jesus Christ as my Saviour." This he did and shortly after that he died.

Now the death of a chief is a very important time. The wailing and crying starts and all the drums start beating incessantly. In such a culture if you don't get involved in this you may be accused of killing the person by witchcraft. But this time it was different. There was a calmness and dignity as they went in procession to the cemetery. Mr Lammond preached the gospel and you could have heard a pin drop. As they stood round the grave they sang, "O God our help in ages past, our hope for years to come". The chief was buried as a Christian and all respected his wishes. God had been gracious to him, but we must remember that it is dangerous to wait till the last hour before we trust the Saviour.

Mr and Mrs Lammond needed a break from the Mission and so they went for a trip round Lake Mweru. They went in the little steel boat called *The Kafwa* (meaning Helper). This had been sent out by Mr Fred Elliot, and supplied by friends in Australia and England. It had come in sections which were transported from the coast then put together at the lakeside. It was driven by an outboard motor.

It was to be a five week trip so they loaded bedding, food, petrol and all necessary supplies. Including their helpers there were five of them and very heavily loaded. They visited Chibambo, Kawama, Mpweto, Luanza and a London Missionary Society station on the lake. They stopped at fishing camps on the lake but only found one Christian in any of these. The lake was unkind to them - they were caught in a thunderstorm and soaked to the skin. They struck rocks and were entangled in weeds, and an old hippo passed close by but did not interfere. Their only loaf of bread was lost in the water and so there was no breakfast that day.

However, reaching Mpweto they were greeted by Mr and Mrs Harry Brown. They spent an enjoyable few days with them and then went on to Luanza. This was a time of relaxation as they enjoyed ten days free from duties. Their last day on Lake Mweru was most enjoyable, the lake so calm this time and a really perfect day for the journey home. They had been advised to take a holiday for the good of their health, and they now felt the better for it.

A conference was held in June 1932 at Sichila's village. It was a beautiful site. They slept in tents and grass shelters and met for teaching under shady trees. There were 14 missionaries who gathered together with national believers. Each party catered for themselves but bread, meat and vegetables were supplied. They met each morning for prayer and in the morning the men and women met separately for discussion. In the afternoon they had a general meeting for Bible teaching where two Africans gave the teaching. In the evening they met round the campfire and had a time of praise, testimonies and choirs. The children had their own services. It was a great time of fellowship as different encampments provided dinner and supper. They took a collection which was sent to the British and Foreign Bible Society.

Mr George O Ratteray had joined the work in 1932 and was there until 1939. He was involved in the school work and biblical teaching. It was his joy to see many trusting the Lord and being baptised. A one legged man at first would have nothing to do with the message because he liked beer too much. However after discussion with his wife they both listened to the gospel and trusted the Saviour.

Sometimes we wonder did those missionaries get any breaks from their work? Miss Woolnough described how she spent the long holiday from school. Packing her bag with some food and clothing she went off itinerating from village to village, walking many miles. Gathering the women together she told them of the love of God. They gave her a room where she could sleep and in the evening she gathered the ladies around the campfire. They ate together and she taught them how to sew but most of all they wanted to hear "the good words".

Mr Stokes went off on a trek to the Livingstone Memorial. With him were Mr Coleman and Mr Barham. This journey is about 350 miles and on the way they visited many villages. Following the pattern of the Lord Jesus they took very little with them, simply accepted the hospitality given to them. They slept in some tiny room, lying on the mud floor; they too gathered round the campfire and taught the people about the Saviour.

All the missionaries made journeys like this on foot reaching out into the villages to tell of the Saviour. The local African evangelists did this also. Miss Fulton tells of one of them who went with his wife on a three month trek into Belgian Congo. They trusted the Lord to supply all their needs, and were well received in the villages. They reached as far as Bunkeya and Koni Hill. It reminds us of those from the early church who went everywhere preaching the gospel!

Mr Stokes tells of walking a short 16 miles to a beautiful riverside village and preaching the gospel. Miss Fraser relates how they made a tour around the lake on foot. They organised camp conferences and over 400 would attend for a week. Mr Lammond told of his first attempt at having a Bible school. It was an experiment for one month with everyone bringing their own food. He said it was heart warming to see the joyful interest shown in the simple things he was able to impart.

During 1935 the hospital continued to expand. Miss Fulton was assisting Miss Fraser. They had an attack of measles followed by pneumonia, which was like a plague among the children in the Luapula valley. Death came to almost every home. The hospital was full and by God's grace they were able to save many lives. The attendance of out-patients had increased from 100 to 180 per day.

Many patients who came had bad burns. This often happens to children who fall into the fire used to cook their food. These ones had burns over large areas of their body which were so painful and had to be dressed frequently. At one time Miss Fraser had three such children in the wards. She had an old gramophone and while dressing the burns she tried to console them by playing music. Sounds like something from the present day? There is nothing new under the sun! Modern treatment for cleaning burns wounds uses another old idea - to introduce maggots into the wounds. Personally I have seen this happen with no other treatment given, and what a beautiful job they made! From time to time cases of smallpox would also appear, and also the dreaded cholera.

Transport in the early days made use of a chair built onto a wheel of a bicycle which was pushed and pulled by two people. Then along came the motorbike and sidecar, and later a motor vehicle came. Mr Lammond told of a unique experience in 1935 of being able to motor from Lobito on the west coast all the way to Mambilima, a little over 2,000 miles of travelling. The truck did so well crossing the mountains, as well as through sand and mud in the plains. Crossing the mountain range they encountered a most vicious storm when they just had to sit still till morning. In 1906 this journey had taken 76 days, now they had covered twice the distance in 16 days.

Cycles – Motor and Pedal

The Monocycle Chair Transport

The greatest difficulty was having to cross their own river, the Luapula. Mr Anton built a raft and Mr Ratteray had a good rope and a large fund of energy. Between them they got the vehicle up the steep banking! The welcome they received was beyond words. The children were great, they sang and jumped for joy, giving both him and Mrs Lammond lumps in their throats!

Mrs Grace Crawford died in 1936. She was a great woman who carried herself with dignity. Miss Woolnough remembered an old elder praying "she was the leader who first came to *seba* (cut a path with a hoe) the pathway for the others". Yes she certainly had put in some good "hoeing".

There was also great excitement that year as Mr Stokes married Miss Ruth Pickering. They were married at Mambilima and the whole village turned out for the occasion. The vast crowd in and around the church building was almost uncontrollable. They continued in the work there until 1949.

In 1937 Mr Ray Smith joined the work at Mambilima and was there until 1942. This strengthened the school work and also the teaching in the villages. He then took up employment and became Principal of the Hodgson Training College.

Mr and Mrs Barham were married at Mambilima in 1937 and Dr and Mrs Mason also had their official wedding here and then a religious one at Chibambo.

Mr and Mrs C F Hogg visited Mambilima and he taught the word of God and conducted conferences in the area. He was a great Bible teacher. Thus the great work continued and many new churches were planted during these years - in Lubundu, Kabundafyela, Nkoma, Mulonga, Matente, Chalwe, Sicibangu, and one at Kolala's village.

CHAPTER 11

The War Years and After

The 1940s began as difficult years while war raged across the world. Many Zambians were called up into active service, but being a Rhodesian Mr Lammond was exempt. There were great shortages of supplies, and communications were limited. But the work at Mambilima forged ahead.

In his energetic and imaginative way Mr Lammond was able to use what was available. He had an untiring thirst for knowledge and he had a sizable library of technical books. These included the following titles "How to make Leather", "How to mend Boots", so that a boot repairing sideline workshop was in constant use. Africans who had lost a leg were fitted out with a wooden one, generally ordered by the government.

Finding suitable disused wheels from old corn mills he mounted them on bearings and from these built a simple lathe. Blind boys were given employment turning the drive wheel. He used this lathe to turn wooden legs for people and wooden legs for chairs! In these days ivory was readily available and he trained boys to turn bracelets, egg cups, salt cellars, beads and paper knives.

He also constructed a 'Heath-Robinson' contraption for retting (shredding) sisal leaves. That task normally took African boys many days to perform. His machine was operated by two blind boys and the retting could be accomplished in minutes. His many practical projects included building a bicycle repair shop, and running trade classes. The zinc dispensary table he made and erected would have been a credit to any hospital.

Mr Lammond provided a translation of the Psalms which was bound into a volume with the New Testament. For many years this was the only part of the Old Testament available for Bemba readers. His interest in languages never flagged; he was keen in his pursuit of idiomatic Bemba right to the end.

He wrote a grammar in Bemba with the modest title "One Hundred Lessons in Bemba". This went through many editions producing thousands of copies. When giving copies to his pupils his one demand was that they would spend as much time doing the lesson as he had preparing it!

Looking forward to the day when electricity would come to the village he had wired his house in readiness. Meantime he installed a diesel engine to drive a dynamo. The same engine worked a pump in the river to fill various concrete tanks with water for houses, school and hospital. He did live to see the day when the government would supply electricity for cookers, fridges and all manner of conveniences.

1940 was the year that the school for blind children was opened at Mambilima. There were only four children at the commencement, but this developed over the years until there were 44 children in 1958.

The numbers attending the schools kept on increasing until in 1945 there were 1030 pupils attending at Mambilima. This was the highest numbers in Zambia. Such large numbers put a great strain on classroom facilities and human resources. Mr and Mrs Stokes told of the great stress that they were under while he was unsuccessfully trying to do the work of two people. Eventually overwork took its toll, and they had to leave the work in 1948 after a severe illness and sadly were not able to return to Zambia. But Mr Stokes had the joy of seeing his pupils doing very well in their exams with a good pass rate. The twenty teachers who sat the government exam were all successful, much to his joy and delight.

In 1944 a terrible fire destroyed the large meeting room which could hold 1,000 people. This is the big disadvantage of a grass roof. It was started deliberately in the middle of the night by a madman. Everything was lost including a lovely organ which was a gift from Miss Habershon. It was a priority to have the meeting room replaced. The new roof needed 900 wooden poles but there was a shortage of wood nearby. The poles were cut in the forest 20 miles away and had to be carried to the site as quickly as possible, for it was imperative that the roof be completed before the rains came. Miss Fraser proved her worth in this situation as she stepped into the breach when this happened and took charge.

Miss Woolnough had seen much blessing among the girls at the school. Not only were they passing their exams but many trusted the Lord and were baptised. She spoke of the happy times that were spent at conferences. At one of these they were outside at the Communion Service under a large mango tree. The silence was suddenly disturbed when a large snake fell out of the tree among the women! The screams and the jumping were a sight to see - for the snake was a thing to avoid!

In 1944 Miss Woolnough left Mambilima for Mansa. It was her desire to be married before she was 70 years old. Having proposed to Mr Sims they were married on the day before her 70th birthday. The Book of Proverbs says that the way of a man with a maid is past finding out, how much more when it is the other way round!

This was also the year when Miss Meryl Shepherd joined the work. She was joined by her sister Elizabeth in 1946 and between them they took responsibility for the school work at Mambilima and district. There was no other school in the Luapula Province offering a full primary school course, so in the boarding school were boys who were selected from the whole province, some having walked 200 miles to come to school.

Mr Stokes and his wife reported that 1945 had been a most stressful year. It began with the State visit of the paramount Chief and finished with the ending of the Great War. The end of the war was a very special occasion. A big Union Jack was raised over the mission. A large crowd gathered to hear the king's speech. Mr Stokes translated the speech into Bemba for the crowd. The national anthem was sung. One boy wrote "Hitler is doomed".

The Sunday service was special. All the benches were taken outside and the service held in the open. The Pathfinder Scouts took part carrying their large Union Jack. The school choir sang. A message of thanksgiving to God was given for His goodness, and to crown it all a trainee teacher gave his life to the Lord Jesus.

In this year another extraordinary service took place. It was taken by an elder called James and his schoolboy son. The son was attending a government school and having trusted the Lord Jesus as his Saviour he wanted to be baptised. He said that he wanted to be baptised as recorded in the Bible, he wanted to be immersed in the water. But this was not the way it was done at the school! This caused a bit of a commotion, however the young man stood firm and he was baptised by immersion.

At the service James went on to speak about Zacchaeus, describing him as a government official who wanted to see Jesus. Forgetting his dignity he ran and climbed a tree to get a good view of Jesus passing. "Can you imagine," he said, "a government official in this country up a tree, looking down and talking with a peasant preacher?" That was how he preached.

In 1946 Miss Stirling came to help Miss Fraser who was failing in health and in 1948 she had to return to the UK. While in Scotland in her late fifties she took her driving licence and then returned to Mansa, travelling with her large vehicle from village to village serving the people. Meryl Shepherd went to Sakeji School to give some help there.

During 1946 Mr Lammond was seriously ill with blood poisoning, yet the potentially serious story has a touch of humour! Dr Dixon was called over from Chibambo to treat the patient. When all attempts to revive him had failed, Dr Dixon decided on a do-or-die emergency treatment. He injected Mr Lammond with a solution of powdered milk because of certain properties it contained. The patient soon came up smiling, none the worse of his experience! His life was spared. Friends told him that he looked like a corpse during the illness. The powdered milk was the same brand that the same Mr Lammond used to make his locally famous ice-cream!

Miss W A R Wagland joined the work at Mambilima and went to Pweto after her first furlough. Mr and Mrs Budge came and worked for some time. This was also the year that Miss Noeline Stockdale arrived and took over the hospital when Miss Fraser went home to the UK.

Thus these turbulent years were blest by the Lord in so many ways for the benefit of so many people in the Luapula valley.

God's Leading
Each person who has come to Zambia as a missionary has a very personal story to tell about how they got there. All those people we have met so far have followed the biblical principle of trusting God with their soul and their life, and also for their daily subsistence. Like Abraham in the Bible when God called him to leave his country, his kindred and his father's house, they too left their home country for another. They use the phrase "Living by Faith" to describe this kind of life.

Miss Elizabeth Shepherd referred to above, who became Betty Lammond, has left on record in a letter to Mr Stunt some of the story of how she heard the call of God. She tells how her parents were devoted Christians who committed every detail of their lives to the will of God. As a young man her father felt the Lord was calling him to overseas service but the way for this did not open up for him. So unknown to anyone he prayed that at least two of his children should become missionaries. The wonder of this was at that time he was not married and had no family. His own family had no idea of his call and this prayer.

Although she had trusted the Lord at the age of four Betty never told anyone about her salvation until she was 18 years old. After taking a degree in mathematics at Nottingham and a teacher training course in Hull she had to go to Holland to get a teaching post. It was there she first made a public confession of faith in the Lord Jesus Christ. Then came the war and she returned to England and found a teaching post in a girls' school.

On talking to a missionary at that time she became aware that God was calling her to give herself to His service, but in what place she wondered. A little later her sister Meryl startled her relatives by telling them that she was giving up her teaching post to take up another form of training. Betty said she had jumped to the conclusion that God was calling her also. When next they were together at home they discussed how the Lord was leading them. This is when they both learned about their father's prayer.

Meryl was the first to be shown where she was needed and wanted, and she sailed for Africa at the end of September 1944. When Meryl wrote home she mentioned the need of a teacher temporarily to replace Mr and Mrs Stokes. So Betty consulted with her church elders and she was commended to go to Mambilima to serve God. She resigned her teaching post, and depending totally on God she too sailed for Zambia in February 1946.

We noted above how Mr and Mrs Stokes could not return to Zambia because of his ill health, but God was there in advance and had already supplied a graduate to take forward His work. God says, "My ways are not your ways," and His ways are "past finding out". It is an almighty, all-knowing God that we serve.

Early Motor Transport

CHAPTER 12

Turbulent Times in the 1950s

Whilst the work at the mission did progress well during the 1950s, the political situation in the country was changing. A wave of nationalism was developing with some evidences of antagonism against the white colonial rulers.

As for wild animals, there is less evidence now of them being a problem. They are still around but much fewer. Monkeys did give lots of trouble, so fishing nets were laid out during the night to catch them. In the early morning loud banging on drums wakened the monkeys who in the confusion ran into the nets and were caught. The resulting soup was great but the meat rather tough! Lions still prowled the district but were much less troublesome. An abundance of crocodiles too were still in the river and caught the unwary. Witchcraft was still very much in evidence in many ways. The belief was and still is in certain quarters that people can change themselves into an animal and kill someone. When a 12 year old girl was caught by a croc and killed, an old man by the name of Kashiba was blamed for it. They said he turned himself into a croc and killed the girl. When the croc was caught and killed the villagers called it "Kashiba"!

A different example concerns an African who died. The coffin was made and the body put inside, then four men carried it to the cemetery for the burial. Near the grave the coffin turned back and returned to the village. The bearers said they had no control over it! It made straight for an old woman and the coffin struck her three times. She then had to walk to the grave and there she died. The bearers said they did not do it - it was the coffin that did it! The old woman was, of course, accused of being a witch! This time the authorities stepped in and the men were charged with causing the death of the old lady.

*   *   *   *   *   *

In 1951 Mr W Lammond discussed with the other missionaries the idea of giving up the work. He was in fact working himself too hard and was mentally exhausted. However he was persuaded by the others to take a break of six months and then return for another term of service. This he agreed to, but stressed that older missionaries should not remain too long on mission stations with the considerable responsibilities involved.

When the Lammonds went on furlough, Mr and Mrs Arthur Morse came from Lwela to relieve them. Rosemary, one of their daughters, was 14 years old at the time. When in Mambilima she asked to be baptised. So along with several Africans she was baptised in the river, thousands of folk gathering to witness a "white" person being baptised the same as a "black" one! What a sight! the dug-out canoes forming a semi-circle in the river to keep the crocs away, the crowds on the bank watching intently, and the elder called Pandawe immersing one after the other, all bearing witness to their faith in the Lord Jesus Christ as their Saviour.

Rosemary remembers the kindness and love shown to her as a child, and to her sister Ruth, by Noeline Stockdale and Cathie Arthur. They got them to help in the hospital and were a great encouragement to them. It was at Mambilima that the seeds were sown for the future and both Ruth and Rosemary entered the nursing profession. Noeline had a wonderful, warm smile. She was so very interested in you as a person - everyone loved her!

Mrs George Lammond tells of the farewell meeting that was held for George and herself after they had gone to Mambilima to give some help there. The hall was packed with over 700 inside and many more outside. Brother Willie Lammond spoke and Ken Kruse and also George. Then they went down to the river where 130 men and women were baptised. Then they had the 'communion service' where at least 600 participated. The meeting finished by singing "When the roll is called up yonder I'll be there". There were many tears as George shook hands with the men while she did the same with the women.

On the 13th December 1952 Mr Willie Lammond's wife Dora passed away. They had been married for 45 years. The funeral service was conducted by Joseph Kaluba, Head Teacher at the school, and Mr Kruse.

The anti-European feeling was growing in strength at this time. In 1953 Mr Lammond was accused of closing the lake to fishing when in fact he had written to the authorities to say that such a step would bring great hardship to the people. Trouble was so bad in the valley that armed forces had to take control for some time. This feeling involved some Christians in the church, and Mr Lammond was accused of getting involved in politics. The ill felling was bad enough to cause a number to separate and start another church in the village. I am glad to say that reconciliation took place and the two churches continue today in happy fellowship with each other.

There were happier occasions too. 1953 was also the year when Mr Lammond and Miss Elizabeth Shepherd were married. I am told it was quite a strange sight for the local folks to see this mature couple walking hand in hand through the village!

To add to this, Mr Lammond received a new car in this year. It was a Ford, supplied by friends in England. When the husband of one of their friends died, the widow had put a notice in the paper that there were to be no flowers at the funeral, but all monies would go to Mr W Lammond, missionary in Africa. "I received £64!" he said, and wondered if this was something unique. The new car was a great blessing, for the journey to Kawama which used to take two days could now be done in two hours!

As more vehicles appeared on the roads there were more accidents. A lorry travelling to Mambilima hit a bridge and plunged over the edge into the river. A first-aider on board was hurt but managed to help the injured. The many injured were brought into the hospital where the staff and the facilities were stretched to the limit for they arrived during the night.

In 1954 Mr and Mrs Jim Ford came to Mambilima. They could not return to French Equatorial Africa as they had wished and offered to join the work here. They fitted in quickly and made swift progress in learning the Bemba Language. As Jim became more fluent in the language his gift as an evangelist came to the fore. He had the joy of seeing many people place their faith in the Lord Jesus Christ.

The school work was progressing, and in 1955 Mrs Lammond became principal of the schools on the mission. This included the primary, middle and upper schools and also the school for the blind. Meryl Shepherd concentrated on the work with the girls. Mr Ford was appointed Manager of Schools for the whole of the district with six primary and five middle schools under his care. He also had a very large teaching staff to supervise which involved him in a steep learning curve!

Miss Stockdale wrote about how busy the hospital was, for they had one epidemic after another. Most days there were over 80 in-patients with mostly whooping cough, measles, malaria and pneumonia all at one time. They thought things were settling down when an epidemic of smallpox broke out. The out-patient department was transferred to the boys' Boarding School and Miss Arthur took charge of this. The staff slept in the hospital so that they were isolated from the village. The 76 patients were all vaccinated and quarantined. The Lord cared for their daily needs in a wonderful way during this time - never once did the meal-barrel run dry! The Christians from the area brought meal, peanuts, meat and firewood each day, much appreciated as practical tokens of Christian grace. The next year there was an epidemic of influenza, which was followed by one of whooping cough. Then fresh cases of smallpox appeared. Although under great pressure the work continued.

When dealing with situations of such poverty and ill health very sad situations are often encountered. Miss Arthur tells of a couple who walked over 50 miles with a sick child on a bicycle. She was their sixth child and all the others had died. This child died three hours after their arrival. They had no relatives, but the Christians gathered round to give comfort. Mr Lammond made the coffin, some of the men dug the grave, Henry Pandawe prayed and they made their way to the cemetery. Henry and Ammon conducted a short service as a few gathered round and lowered the little coffin into the grave. Such sad scenes were not uncommon in those days. But at the same time there was a great wave of blessing in all aspects of the work. As the gospel was preached people believed the message and committed themselves to Jesus Christ as their Lord and Saviour.

The Christians had a joyful surprise one day when a soldier serving in the Northern Rhodesian regiment arrived at Mambilima. While he had been serving with his regiment in Malaya he heard the message of the gospel, believed and was baptised. Here he was now returning to his homeland as a Christian with a letter of commendation from the believers in Malaya. God's ways are far greater than we can imagine!

Mr W T Stunt from Echoes of Service visited in 1955 and saw the extent of the work. There were now 18 churches associated with CMML in the Luapula valley with over 1,800 in fellowship. There were also twelve schools with twelve trained teachers along with many support teachers and 2,500 pupils. At Mambilima School they had 600 pupils with 60 in the school for the blind. The Sunday School had 400 pupils and there were four evangelists active in the gospel locally.

There was great rejoicing when the new chief Mulundu became a Christian. His immediate predecessor had been bitterly opposed to the Mission and was a heavy drinker. It is not easy to be a Chief and a Christian at the same time as there are still many cultural problems associated with chieftainship. However this man's wife was also a Christian and was a great help to him.

* * * * * *

Sometimes being in a foreign land produces nostalgia and a great longing for home, a longing to breath the native air and to hear one's own native dialect. Meryl Shepherd wrote: "It is very beautiful here, especially in the early morning and late evening, but the bright sunshine kills the colours. The green grass is coarse and full of creepy-crawlies. It is difficult to climb the hills because the undergrowth is too thick and may hide snakes. There are very few walks that one can take given the time available. I have learnt to accept and enjoy it as it is." Then she added, "But believe me, there is no country that I have ever seen so beautiful as that small island that we call home!" I am reminded of the words from the poet,

> *"Breathes there a man with soul so dead,*
> *Who never to himself has said,*
> *This is my own, my native land."*

The apostle Paul thought of his home city Tarsus as "no mean city". Yet surely in the heart of every Christian there is the longing for their eternal home - in the Father's house!

In 1956 there was great excitement when the first edition of the

Bemba Bible was produced. It was the result of years of labour in translation. Mr Lesley Barham had typed the full script of the Bible on an old typewriter no less than three times and checked it thoroughly. Now the complete Word of God was available in the mother tongue of the people - what a treasure! Mr Barham went on to produce the Braille Bible later that year - a great help for those who could not see.

Mr Ford reported that 1957 was a year of great blessing, a year of progress and reaping. There were no less than 117 baptisms. The gospel was preached daily at the hospital and great crowds gathered to hear. Mothers come in their hundreds to the out-patient department, lepers hear it in their colony, and any who will listen hear about the Lord Jesus.

The new building at the hospital was progressing and taking shape nicely. Mr Lammond said that the nursing sisters will not know themselves once they get in! They were supposed to accommodate 40 in-patients, but last week they had 74. He said, "Don't ask me where they slept – on beds, under beds and on the floor, I suspect."

The new building was completed before the rains came, and during this year the rains were excessive. They were cut off from Chibambo and Kawama. The river had risen 70 feet above normal and was so turbulent that the river pontoon could not be used for crossing. The road between Mansa and the Copperbelt was closed, and mail had to come via diversions of hundreds of miles.

1958 was the Diamond Jubilee of the start of the work at Mambilima. Another church was commenced and they now had 21 churches in this year. Mr Lammond and Mr Ford were involved in running the Central African Broadcasting Station which was based at Mambilima and broadcasted on a regular basis. Recordings were made by the boys in the school for the blind.

During the wet season there is always the great danger of an electric storm. These are magnificent to watch as the sky is lit up with an array of brilliant colours and the thunder rolls incessantly, but it is highly dangerous. Jim Ford told of such a storm on February 7th 1959. It struck both the upper and lower primary schools and caused severe damage to the property. Four of the girls were hit, one being killed instantly while the other three recovered from the delayed shock.

The storm had struck suddenly while the girls had gone to collect water running off the iron roof, thus exposing themselves to the elements. The parents of the girl who died had just lost their oldest son while at school only one month previously. The trauma to the family was tremendous. The father was not a Christian and said that as a family they were bewitched. He had his daughter buried immediately, wrapped only in a mat, and refused to let his friends grieve and mourn at his house. This is most unusual for an African.

The three-classroom block at Mulundu's village was also struck and was on fire. Jim Ford ran the half mile through the storm. They were able to able to pull out all the desks and equipment before it became a raging inferno and was razed to the ground. The church building was used as temporary accommodation.

Later in 1959 a "state of emergency" arose in the work in the Luapula. Greater demands were being made by the government to increase the quality and the amount of education. Things had been brought to a head by a violent nationalistic group who were demanding that the government should act. The police brought the lady missionaries from Kawama along to Mambilima for their safety while they were patrolling regularly.

The government wanted to raise the standard of education, but there were difficulties meeting the demands because of the lack of trained teachers. The missionaries were anxious because the Roman Catholic Church was pushing forward to take over the

CMML schools. CMML has had the school work in the valley for 60 years, and most of the believers had come to Christ through either the school or the medical work. They did not want to lose the benefit of the good work done by the early pioneers. A vigorous protest was lodged which was successful. It was important to grasp these opportunities when they came as they would not arise again.

So a period of great turbulence had come and gone, but by the grace of God the work moved forward in the hands of dedicated men and women who had been willing and courageous to give themselves to it.

CHAPTER 13

Tensions in the 60s

In the years that led up to independence great tensions arose in the country and the Luapula Province was not exempt. The nationalistic element caused many problems which brought foreign missionaries into the limelight. On one occasion in 1960 the cattle pen at Johnston Falls was burned down, roasting alive around 24 cows. Mr Lammond was unable to count the carcases because of the heat. Some of the calves were scorched and it was doubtful if they would live. The police took the matter in hand and the mission came under police protection.

As a result of the antagonism the police opened a station in the valley and a curfew was put in place. In the Copperbelt it was reported that the people were prevented from getting to a Billy Graham rally. Cars were smashed and the police had to use tear gas to break up a riot. A Zambian Air Force plane patrolled overhead.

The intimidation continued and Mr Ford made a special appeal for prayer for the Lord's people in the Luapula valley. The enemy was seeking to destroy God's work in the churches, hospitals and schools. The teachers of the blind pupils were intimidated by a large crowd who accused the missionaries of trying to upset the "master plan" for gaining control of the country. They said that if they were reported again for their behaviour they would close the CMML schools and stop the Christians from gathering. They were told in turn that the missionaries were not involved in politics and were subject to "the powers that be" whichever type of government was in control, black or white.

Mr Ford's special prayer for this situation was "that we may come forth as pure gold". It was a very difficult time and all the newspapers carried stories of the problems in the country, especially in the Luapula Province.

All this had an effect on the spiritual work. People were afraid of being seen coming to church services. There were few conversions and baptisms. Politically, things on the surface seemed to quieten down but underneath there was much unrest. I remember Mr Jim Kennedy at that time in Scotland speaking of "The Wind of Change in Zambia".

But amidst all the problems, life must go on. There was the great rage of the hula-hoops. This seemed to be pandemic among the children. The record was reported to be 13,000 spins around the body – incredible! It was even reported that some of the missionaries got involved in this sport! Do not ask who they were!

Jim Ford kept a pet monkey, a delightful little thing. It went from house to house and would eat what it was given. It is said that it went through the window into Meryl Shepherd's house and drank her tea when she was not looking. Well missionaries must have some relaxation!

One day the cook came to Mr Lammond and complained that his dog Caesar had bit him on the tummy. The story was that the cook had opened up the organ to play a tune and out jumped two mice on to his lap. Quick as a flash the dog leaped upon the mouse and in addition to getting the mouse it took a bite of the cook's midriff. The cook got the other mouse!

During these difficult days the missionaries kept in frequent contact with each other. There were regular visits between Kawama, Chibambo and Mambilima which meant journeys by car and canoe. These could be made in a journey time of around two hours each way. Birthdays were days for special celebration and on Mr Lammond's 83rd birthday they had a big party. The children were included and there was cake and candles, Mr Lammond's famous ice cream with jelly, and then the evening included a fireworks display on the football field.

Mambilima was a very busy place with many visitors coming and going. Some came for a week at a time, others only for an overnight stay. Betty Lammond's visitors' book records that in the month of January 1962 around 30 different people visited Mambilima. Much work was involved arranging food, beds and accommodation especially when shopping was almost impossible. However I am told that Meryl Shepherd could get twenty slices of meat out of a tin of corned beef!

Although Mr Lammond was 83 he was still busy. After a storm had brought down the electric cables he was seen up a ladder fixing them together again. Then when the roof needed repair he was up on the roof in the thick of the work. That was his style.

He decided that his car needed a re-spray and so he constructed a pump which would give enough pressure to work a spray gun. It was hard work operating the pump manually so that the people operating it had to do it in relays of 10 minutes at a time. The colour scheme turned out to be cream on the top and maroon on the bottom. The car became easily seen and well known in the valley.

New people joined the work in 1960. Miss Irene Mann, a nurse/midwife gave valuable service until 1965 when she left to marry Mr Alan Gammon and moved to South Africa. Dr Keir Howard and Dorothy Howard joined the staff and were at Mambilima until 1964 when they moved further up country. Dorothy too was a nurse/midwife and they both gave valuable service in the medical work.

Because of the unrest in the valley and the danger of arson attacks the missionaries were encouraged to re-roof their houses with a more permanent material. In the main they used metal ("tin") for this and in 1960 they re-roofed five houses. It was a lot of hard work to convert from grass to metal. Jim Ford decided to use asbestos for his house and it was completed in 1961. These materials made the houses much safer but very much hotter, and when it rains it is impossible to hear oneself speaking inside!

Jim Ford celebrated his 40th birthday on the 12th April 1961. Now he felt really old! Betty and Will Lammond gave him a walking stick and a book called *The Best is yet to be — a tonic for the elderly*! One does need a sense of humour to keep sane!

Letters arrive from many different sources, some making you sad and others glad. Yet another group cause you to smile or laugh out loud. This one was received from a student taking a college course on carpentry:

> "I have not decided either to come back for the instruction course or not. My aim at past was to come back for instruction course, but this time I am doubting. At any rate I may. And therefore I conclude that I am not sure about this."

Well I trust the dear fellow made up his mind eventually!

The work at the hospital was still going ahead. New buildings were being used and people were being blessed. Patients were hearing the gospel relayed to them from tapes. Miss Stockdale in charge was a woman of outstanding ability and had an aura about her person. She was indeed feared by many in some ways. She was ably assisted by Cathie Arthur and others from time to time.

Governor Sir Evelyn Hone visited the mission and village in 1962. There were 450 children in the school then. The blind children demonstrated their baskets, trays and knitting. At this time Miss Mann took her language exam and was successful.

Mr and Mrs Ford had a bad accident with their car in 1962 when taking their children to school at Sakeji. Dorothy was badly injured - her leg was broken and took a long time to heal. In 1963 Jim had a bad attack of jaundice, and cartilage trouble with his right knee. He was also losing the use of his right hand and had to use his left hand for writing. As a result of their ill health they decided to leave Mambilima and they then settled in Kabwe.

The political unrest continued especially among the youth of the country. However the work of the Lord continued unabated. In one of the villages a crowd of around 700 gathered to witness ten believers being baptised. The audience was quiet and orderly with no opposition at all despite the tension in the country. Meryl Shepherd also told of some blind boys and girls being baptised.

Giving to the Lord in these days was much less than normal and this was noticeable in the support given to the evangelists. It was difficult to make a stand for the Lord. Many years earlier Mr Lammond came upon a wedding in a village. The custom in such a situation is to give a monetary gift, however instead Mr Lammond gave the couple some "words of wisdom". Now 45 years later the then bridegroom met Mr Lammond and told him who he was. He also told him that he had now received the greatest gift of all – he had trusted the Lord and had the gift of eternal life. The Bible tells us to "cast your bread upon the waters, and you shall find it after many days" (Ecclesiastes 11.1).

Much unrest and many problems were also being met over the border in the Congo. Refugees were leaving and flooding into Zambia from across the river. It was reckoned there were 22,000 of them. This put an extra strain on a country already under great political stress. The missionaries responded in whatever ways they could to give help to these displaced persons, for the message of Christ Jesus involves bringing the love of God in every practical way possible.

1964 was a historic year in the history of Zambia. On the 25th October Zambia became the ninth African state to gain independence from the British Crown. In the capital city, Lusaka, a large crowd gathered at Independence Stadium and a huge copper torch was lit on a hill overlooking the city.

Mary, the Princess Royal, representing the Queen gave the Instruments of Independence to Kenneth Kaunda, the new President. The people shouted *Kwatcha* meaning a New Dawn. The Union Jack flag was lowered and the Red, Black, Green and Orange flag of Zambia was raised as the Princess read a message from the Queen.

The change-over was conducted in a very peaceful manner and the troubles which many had feared never materialised. In 1965 the new government began taking over the responsibilities for education. Samfya, Lwela and Mansa Schools were the first to be taken over, and Mambilima followed soon after. Mr Ford was given the responsibility for the handover. Mr Lammond said that now he was no longer able to do his full share of the work and he no longer went out of the station into the villages. He lamented that there was a great need for someone to do the village work.

The hospital was as busy as ever. Cathie Arthur wrote of the joy of triplet boys being born, small but healthy. The mother had come to the hospital in a canoe, travelling from 9am and arriving at 5.30pm. The first child was born three hours later. The last triplets before these were girls who were now five years of age and doing well.

There was a bad accident when the drunk driver of a bus crashed his vehicle. This happened during the night and the hospital was busy all night till morning with the injured. Fortunately no one was killed.

Evidence of hostility was still seen towards the African brothers and sisters who made a stand for Christ. Ba Pandawe, one of the local elders had his house and kitchen burned down, then that of his son, then the next day that of his daughter-in-law. But he and his wife stood firm for the Lord amidst the persecution.

In 1967 Mr Lammond recounts a heart warming experience.

"A deputation from the Congolese churches had come to discuss some problems. One of the visitors was a middle aged man with the kindliest smile I ever saw on an African. I did not know him but had heard he had suffered much for being a Christian leader. When he mentioned the name of his father, a picture sprang up before me of a camp fire in an African village and myself a very green missionary in 1902. The headman of the village told us he had decided to put both feet in the Jesus way and not to walk on two paths.

"Another picture came equally vividly before me. It is many years later and I am kneeling in a hut. The same headman is lying on a mat on a mud floor, hardly able to speak, the last spark of life flickering away as he looks at me, and with his finger raised he points upwards to heaven. His feet had kept the Jesus way right to the end!

"And now here was his son, his whole countenance beaming with the love of the Lord! I could not resist the impulse to break into his speech and tell the elders what his father had said to me 64 years ago – and fully implemented in his life and work."

Mr Lammond became ill shortly after this and went to the Copperbelt for help. His desire and wish was to die at Mambilima and the Lord granted him his desire. On Saturday 24th February 1968 he was taken into the presence of the Lord.

CHAPTER 14

The End of an Era

Mr Lammond's great desire was that he should die in Zambia. He had paid many visits to the UK but could not stand the cold. He had just spent some months on the Copperbelt because of illness, but his desire was to get back to Mambilima. His last journey to Mansa was by plane. Dr McColl says their last sight of him was of a rather frail old gentleman settling himself into his place on a DC 3 plane, looking about him missing nothing of interest, and with an almost boyish smile on his face as his seat belt was fastened.

It was rather fitting that he should finish his "trek" by such modern means. He was one of the very few old timers who had been able to adapt to the many changing circumstances as the violent winds of change blew across Africa. Here was a realist who saw people and things as they are and was not disillusioned but only challenged to renewed effort and constancy. He showed that the faith of our fathers is the faith for today.

There had been torrential rains in the valley and it was impossible for W L to make the last 60 miles by road from Mansa to Mambilima. But at the right moment the rains eased, the road became passable and he came home. It is not really surprising that the Lord should arrange the last stage of such an ordered life.

Mr Lammond passed peacefully into the presence of his Lord

on Saturday, February 24th 1968 at 11.45pm. The meetings were held as normal on Sunday morning. Miss Stockdale went to the nearest doctor 60 miles away and gave the news to fellow workers and colleagues at Kawama.

The funeral service was at 3pm on Sunday. There was a huge crowd of over 1,000 people inside and outside the hall. A reverent silence descended upon the congregation and the presence of the Lord was felt. Mr Arthur Morse gave an appreciation of the life of William Lammond, and four others spoke of what this man had done in the strength of the Lord for the area and for its people.

The coffin was taken in procession to the burial ground. The earthly remains of William Lammond were committed to the ground, awaiting the great day of resurrection. The wonderful message of Christian hope was spoken at that graveside. He was with the Lord and for him it was far better. Truly he could say, "I have fought a good fight, I have finished my course, I have kept the faith."

Reflecting on Mr Lammond's life Dr Eddie McColl said, "When many are turning aside or even dropping out of the race, it has been a high privilege to know as a friend this one who set out on the right road, kept on it, and whom we saw 'makin a guid feenish'."

Here was a man who with a twinkle in his eye said in a husky voice as he cleared his throat, "Ninety-one years is a terribly long time to live. I'm almost ashamed to be here, but if I've done any little good then 'not unto us, O Lord, not unto us, but to Thy name give glory'."

Mr Lammond once wrote with typical modesty, "Old-timers are often asked for adventure stories. I can supply nothing out of the ordinary apart from brushes with hippos, being knocked down by a lion, having a snake spit in my eye, having been three times in canoes which have turned over, and having my house burnt down accidentally. Mine has been a quiet and a good life, and I thank God for His protecting care and for permitting me to take some part in leading men and women to Christ, and in building up some churches of believing Christians here in Central Africa during the past 64 years."

On another day he had chuckled heartily when someone asked him if our friends who had already gone to be with the Lord could communicate with each other. He said, "If they can they'll surely be asking, 'Where is old W L that he's not yet here?'."

He had survived all his original missionary colleagues and modestly shrugs off suggestions that he had more than earned his MBE, the Royal Africa Society Bronze Medal and King Albert of Belgium's Pioneer Medal. He was more proud to produce his licence to practise dentistry in Zambia!

Wm Lammond and his MBE and African Medals

Condolences came flooding in to Mrs Lammond. A telegraphic message was received from the President of Zambia:

> "The news of the death of Mr William Lammond has come to us as a shock. The whole country will certainly miss him. Mr Lammond's contribution in the field of mission work and education will be long

remembered. He came to this country at the turn of the century and has since then worked hard and unselfishly for the development of our country. His work on the grammar of one of our languages bears testimony to his zeal for wanting to know the people of this country. On behalf of the Government and the People of the Republic of Zambia, and indeed on my own behalf, I send our deepest and very sincere condolences to the bereaved."

Someone who worked with him for many years paid this tribute to him: "He was a great man and a straight man - one of those unswervingly righteous Scottish characters whom one can only admire - and sometimes fear."

He was undoubtedly a man of great integrity, but he could be autocratic, obstinate and even difficult. But there was another side to his character. He had a mischievous, almost impish, sense of humour and a great love of children with whom he was always thoroughly at home.

So with his passing on from earth to heaven we come to the end of an era, as the beloved people of the Luapula did on that February day in 1968.

CHAPTER 15

Without a Male Missionary in the 70s

For 68 years Mr Lammond had laboured among the Lunda people. Now in a new decade there were no male missionaries over a stretch of 80 miles where many CMML churches exist. Mr Lammond had prayed for a young man to come to serve God in the Luapula, but this was not to be.

Such is the culture that without a male in charge there is a perceived weakness. This weakness was felt in the churches where some individuals like Diotrophes of old wanted to "have the pre-eminence" (see 3 John v.9). There were those who wanted to appoint a "Messenger" to the churches. Some wanted to appoint a pastor, to have a more organized structure and to have a leader.

During these difficult days they were grateful for the help of Jim Kennedy from Mansa. He came to help them on a regular basis. Once a month the elders met for discussion and teaching, and Jim attended these meetings to teach especially the principles of church gathering as given in the New Testament. The Lord's goodness was evident and although at one point eight churches broke away from the others, the work remained firm. In the same year other churches were commenced.

In 1968 the name of the village was changed from Johnston Falls to Mambilima Falls, the name which had been suggested by William and Betty Lammond. Later that year the word 'Falls' was dropped and from then on the village has been known simply as Mambilima.

It was noticeable around this time that the ladies in the Mission were under great pressure and also some danger because of attacks and thieving. During the year two men walked into Noeline and Cathie's house with a knife, a rope and a gun, demanding money. A shot was fired and the bullet entered the wood of the hallstand but fortunately no one was hurt.

Cathie Arthur and Noeline Stockdale, 1968

In 1971 thieves broke into the office at the hospital. One of the thieves stood outside with a bright light while others worked inside. They took the safe outside the building still bolted to its large concrete block foundation. It was found lying over the handles of a wheelbarrow which belonged to Noeline! After lugging it all the way outside they must have let it fall on their fingers. There was blood everywhere! They left it and fled - with nothing but bloodied fingers to show for their burglary. God is good to those who trust and serve Him. He also betimes makes the mischief of evil men rebound on their own heads as it says in Psalm 17.6 (or on their fingers in this case!).

The next day they had a severe storm which blew off the roofs of some of the houses. The headteacher's house also collapsed injuring two people.

The next year thieves broke into Meryl's house. They threw her to the ground and then stole a radio which was a gift from the President. Fortunately Meryl was kept from serious injury. Such thieving was a regular occurrence and many nights their sleep was disturbed with thieves trying to enter their houses. On one occasion they stole the glass from the windows by taking out the new putty just applied for glazing.

In 1973 Noeline's car was stolen and wrecked. This happened a second time some years later and thieves also smashed Margaret Jarvis's windscreen.

After the attempt to steal the safe at the hospital Noeline tried to make it more secure. She had it cemented right into the wall. All was well until 1978 when the thieves struck again. This time they used dynamite and blasted it out of the wall. They had been tipped off that the wages for the staff had been collected from Mansa so they struck at what they thought was the right time. But in the over-ruling goodness of the Lord the wages had been put in a drawer beside the safe but not in it. The staff on duty were petrified during the attack, but gathered stones and threw them at the would-be thieves as they escaped.

They went off with this huge, heavy load and took it down to the river. There they loaded it onto a canoe and started out to cross to Congo on the other side. You may guess what happened! The load was too heavy for the canoe and it promptly sank in the middle of the river - where it lies to this day! The staff received their wages intact, and "He who sits in the heavens laughs" at them, to quote another Psalm (2.4).

Morag Anthony from Scotland arrived in 1970 and remained until 1984. She related how the Lord called her to the mission field. It was through Tom Moses of Brazil giving an address from Isaiah chapter 6, when she was challenged by the words, "Who will go for us?" The answer, "Here am I send me!" She found her answer in coming to Mambilima.

In 1974 Margaret Jarvis came to Mambilima. She had been on a contract as a nurse/midwife at a government mine hospital and had visited Mambilima. There she felt the call to full time service at the Mission. In 1981 she had to return to Scotland because of severe and repeated attacks of malaria. However in 1998 she returned to Mambilima as Mrs Margaret Muir.

Malaria was very common among the missionaries in these days. Among the many reasons for this was night time disturbances often because of thieving, and also they were regularly on call. This meant they had to be escorted to the hospital during the night, the time when mosquitoes are at their most active. Repeated malarial attacks resulted from lack of sleep and having to go out at these more dangerous times.

In 1972 a double Jubilee Celebration for Mrs Anton and Miss Mitchell was held in Mambilima. A service of thanksgiving was held in Noeline's house. It was a great weekend of celebration among the 27 missionaries who were there. They came from Pweto in Congo, Chibambo, Kawama, Mulundu, Mansa and Luwela. What a great time of fellowship they had. One can just imagine the cacophony as all the various mixed dialects of the English language competed with each other!

Mission Medic-Air, a charitable organisation, had taken an interest in children with physical handicaps at the Mambilima School for the handicapped. They said that they would build an airstrip at the village to enable a visiting doctor to fly into the village. In due course a site was given for this purpose at the top of the village, a flat area about a mile long. It took some years to complete but by 1978 a small plane was flying into Mambilima regularly.

The school for the physically handicapped was taking in increasing numbers of children. Noeline relates how touching it was to see the lame, halt and blind all coming to the meetings of the church, many of them able to 'walk' only on their hands and knees. German doctors at the hospital at Mbereshi, 80 miles north, have helped many of these children with corrective surgery. The children can be away for as long as six months having this treatment. Also, with the advent of a plane, Mr George Adams, an orthopaedic surgeon at the mine hospital in Luanshya has taken a number of children there for operations. Many children benefited from this and are now able to walk and wear shoes.

Yet another problem arose in the village and surrounding areas, an epidemic of rabies in the dog population. Officers were sent out by the authorities to shoot the dogs. At the hospital vaccinations were given to those at risk. The vet who came to get his vaccination had 17 dead dogs in the back of his Land Rover!

The hospital was always busy and the beds were always full. Two patients were admitted with bites from crocodiles and miraculously had survived. These wounds always took a long time to heal since the teeth of the crocs are filthy and cause much infection. There were another two patients with fish bites. Life was varied and never dull!

Cathie reported that in 1971 there were 3,161 patients who had attended the hospital, including 261 maternity cases. Many more patients attended clinics. Each one who came received a copy of the Gospel of Luke - with their patient number written inside it. It serves as their treatment card and encourages care in the proper use of the book.

During 1972 Cathie reported on the coldest day she ever knew in Africa. It was a day in June. On duty that day she wore heavy shoes, a heavy cardigan and an anorak. "It's a bleak country without the sun," she said. One of the female orderlies wore a pair of jeans and a wee short skirt, a big cardigan and a woolly scarf tied round her head. A senior orderly wore a thick jumper with a polo neck over his face and ears. Another tied a scarf round his nose to keep it warm. They had such a laugh it took the chill out of the morning!

There was much excitement in 1973 when Betty Lammond was decorated by President Kenneth Kaunda at the State House in Lusaka. She was honoured with the Order of Distinguished Service, the Fourth Division and therefore entitled to use the letters MDS after her name. Two of the Zambian newspapers carried the story. Zamu Zulu, a reporter with the Sunday Times of Zambia wrote in the 8th June 1975 issue that she was "Queen of the Luapula". Here was this "old lady" of 62 years who had "reigned" for 29 years in the Luapula. Mama Betty Lammond, the upright and elegant lady who looked much younger than her years had given outstanding service to the country. He described her as a staunch missionary, qualified mathematician and vernacular linguist. Indeed Mrs Lammond was all this and more, rolled together into one petite Briton.

When someone asked her how many years she was prepared to remain and work with these "destitutes", she replied, "For as long as I am alive." Then the old lady added, "It's not what one looks like on the outside that matters - but what she or he has inside."

More developments took place in the valley. A new tarred road was laid from Mambilima to Mansa. This made such an improvement to speed and comfort when taking patients to the hospital there. Then the government set out to bring electricity to the village but the hardness of the rock formation was a big problem. Their drills could not bore through it and they had to use dynamite to blast a way through. Eventually they were successful and the village had the new joy of being connected to the hydro-electric power station at Musonda Falls.

During these years food was in short supply and it was difficult to get essential supplies. The missionaries were so grateful to those who sent out parcels of food. The shelves in the shops in town were empty. Medicines too were in short supply. Margaret Jarvis tells of being down to the very last box of chloroquine when a fresh supply arrived. The Lord's timing is always perfect.

Building work continued at the hospital during these years. Mission Medic-Air built a new U-shaped block which included a children's ward, under 5s clinic, an X-ray department, a laundry, a food store and a kitchen. These new facilities were great and made working conditions so much better for the staff. They still waited however, to be connected to the electricity supply and to have running water, but this was to come.

It is always a great privilege to be able to show the love of God in a practical way and to tell others of the Saviour. That is one of the reasons for all that has been done at Mambilima and elsewhere. One day a young girl was admitted with a snake bite. Sadly she had been taken first to the witchdoctor and given village medicine. She was now very ill. As all the relatives gathered around her bed, the story of how Jesus loved little children was told. As prayer was being made the little child slipped out of this life into eternity! Oh how important it is to be ready before that time comes for us all.

There was an outbreak of typhoid at Mwense secondary school and Cathie and Noeline were kept busy with this - 22 boys were very ill and one died.

Many of the young men and women in the valley were taken into National Service. Conditions there are very difficult especially for the women. The training is very rigorous and hard and the girls are often weak through lack of food. Those who are believers need a lot of support to resist the great temptations to fall into sinful practices and immoral lifestyles.

Witchcraft is still a big problem in the valley. These nefarious practices were now being made illegal. Zambian government officials in Mansa held a meeting to explain the new Zambian laws particularly about witchdoctors. Some were making big money and one was reported to have three cars! The law said that such practices are illegal and must be reported. A local witchdoctor had been ordered to leave the district because of his behaviour, and Meryl Shepherd told how a middle aged woman on hearing this news did a little dance - in spite of being a size 20!

Jim and Margaret Hopewell and their daughter Christine from Glasgow visited Mambilima in 1978. It was their first visit. Eventually they arrived by air at Mansa and travelled by road to Mambilima. Jim describes their introduction: "If you do not see creepy crawlies it is easier to accept them. So before going into a room at night, put your hand round the door and switch on the light and give them a chance to disappear!"

They were assured by one of the missionaries that there were no snakes around. Since this news came from a reliable source they relaxed. Next morning they were greeted by a houseboy proudly holding up the snake he had killed on the veranda!

On a first visit one is always cautious about food and what new things you eat. Having tucked into a main course of roast beef, potatoes and vegetables they were asked if they enjoyed it? "Yes, yes," they said, "lovely meal." The reply? "Well it was goat meat you ate!" - a first time for everything.

Preparing for bed one night there was an emergency. A family arrived from a distance with a young man draped over a bicycle. He had a strangulated hernia. Urgent discussions were overheard among the nurses. He must go to Mansa at once. Who will go and take him? Well to his horror Jim was told by Noeline that he was the one who was delegated to go along with Margaret Jarvis (now Margaret Muir).

They got into the Morris 1100 estate car, Jim in front, the two men in the back and Margaret at the wheel. It was intense darkness, no street lights, only the stars above as they started on the 60 mile journey. The roads were dirt roads full of potholes, the patient seriously ill in the back, groaning and moaning all the way. It was a new experience for Jim - and not to be recommended.

It took about two hours to reach the hospital. It was a great relief to everyone when they arrived safely. Noeline had supplied a flask of tea. Exhausted they drank it, had a biscuit, and then turned around and drove back to Mambilima. On route they saw many pairs of eyes shining in the dark, one pair was big and blue, but they did not stop to investigate their owner. Arriving back at 2am they gave God thanks for His protection and fell into bed to enjoy the rest that sleep brings to the weary.

Throughout these years the teaching of many children in the schools and Sunday Schools continued and in fact increased. Early morning classes were well attended. Also many people were attending church services freely. There was perfect liberty to continue the work of the gospel in the valley. In 1979 fourteen men and eleven women were baptised.

Joyce Ramsay joined the work at Mambilima in 1979 and continued till 1981. A Dutch physiotherapist called Jan Schrame also came. He was there for around three years and married a Zambian girl. Another phase of the work was thus completed and God has been glorified in it.

CHAPTER 16

Activities in the 80s

Many visitors from overseas and also from Zambia were coming and going in the seventies and eighties. Mr Carl Simmons was from Bermuda and the folks in the valley loved his preaching. He always brought greetings and gifts from the people of distant Bermuda.

The completion of the tar road to Mansa made travel much easier. Before that, in the dry season you got dirt in your hair and teeth and very filthy clothes - you just wanted a bath. In the wet season the road was like a skating rink so you skidded and slithered the whole journey.

Mr and Mrs Andrew Gray from Glasgow came and he gave helpful teaching in the churches. Mrs Gray was overcome by the culture shock as she went for a walk in the village with Margaret, not an unusual reaction when faced for the first time with such poverty and primitive living conditions.

Joyce Ramsay tells how she learned the Bemba language. Betty and Meryl gave her lessons using Mr Lammond's text book. Betty was a real stickler for grammar and pronunciation, and there was never an excuse good enough for not doing her homework! However she was always quick to heap on praise if the learner got it right!

Margaret Jarvis tried to prepare Joyce for sitting her driving test. She patiently showed her how to reverse her Isuzu truck between barrels laid out on the ground. Margaret was horrified how much she kept hitting the barrels, but managed to keep from complaining too much. It was not her fault that she failed her test in Mansa. One of the pilots of the plane said she should have gone in to the test with a sack of potatoes for the examiner and she would have passed no bother! Joyce would not do this and so remained without a Zambian driving licence.

It was Joyce's turn to be horrified watching Margaret doing dental extractions so calmly and efficiently. Because of Joyce's great dislike of dentists she could never take on the task of extracting teeth!

In those days there were people who still tried to disrupt the work. Thieves again tried to break into Noeline's house, fired a gun and shot and injured a boy. Thieves also stole the water pump from the river so again water had to be carried up from the river to the houses and hospital.

Disease was still rampant in the area with many little ones dying of measles and malnutrition. In 1982 they had a cholera epidemic in the area. There were 137 cases of which eleven died, including two dead on arrival. All the beds allocated for the emergency were occupied. The government sent in their special team to help with the outbreak. All patients were given intravenous fluids and tetracycline and were able to go home in five days. All the villagers were given tetracycline and a cholera injection. This was a big task and put a great strain on the facilities. Cathie records that the Lord gave them strength throughout the epidemic and also to treat the widespread eye infections in the valley.

The next year there was another cholera epidemic 100 miles to the north and ten had died. There was great fear that it would spread again and so they vaccinated thousands in the area to try to prevent this. As a result of this epidemic the meetings of the church were curtailed. There was no Communion Service between January and April because of the danger of spreading the disease.

Betty wrote of the amazing spread of the gospel in the last 85 years. This was largely due to how the African believers witnessed to their fellows. Although many were not particularly gifted they went on steadily and faithfully telling their fellow villagers of the Saviour. People looked at them and saw the message backed up by the change which the love of God had brought into their lives. Their behaviour and attitudes were different - they went out of their way to help their neighbours now.

By 1982 there were 41 churches in the area and many would have congregations of over 200. The church elders from the area met once a month for fellowship and teaching. Jim Kennedy continued to come from Mansa to give some of the teaching on these occasions and his wise counsel was greatly appreciated.

* * * * * * * *

At this time the mission station was staffed by mainly mature ladies. It might be worth asking what they did for some recreation?

First there was the daily devotional time and the reading of God's Word. Then the radio would be tuned in, especially to the BBC World Service news programmes. Of course there was no television and no telephones in these days. Letters were written home; Betty and Meryl wrote a letter to their father and mother every week. Letters from home were eagerly waited for and highly prized. Newspapers from home were at least one month out of date, but still devoured from cover to cover. Margaret Jarvis always looked forward to the Dundee published *Sunday Post* with all its local news and gossip, and of course the new episodes of *The Broons* and *Oor Wullie*. Her mother faithfully sent this out to Zambia every week.

Then there was the weekly "Scrabble Fixture". I am told that this was something to behold! Betty, Meryl, Noeline and Cathie were all such serious, capable players. There were these four mature ladies seated round the table, dictionaries at the ready to settle any doubts or disputes. The rules of the game had to be strictly obeyed, absolutely no cheating allowed! Christian grace prevented them from over-heated exchanges and from coming to blows with each other!

A fellowship meal was regularly held in one of the houses. The table was laid with a clean, freshly ironed tablecloth. The finest bone china and cutlery was carefully set in place as in an English stately home. Each stood in reverence behind their chair while thanks was given to God for the food about to be received, then sat down to enjoy the meal served - and eaten with great relish. When available, little treats would surprise the guests, and the evening was rounded of with a good British cup of tea. All agreed that God is good!

* * * * * * *

Mark Davies arrived from Wales in February 1983. Here was a young man who was going to be an asset to the work. He commenced to learn the Bemba language and at the same time started doing many of the urgent practical tasks around the mission. One of these was to put in the plumbing and electric wiring in the new ward that had been built at the hospital for the children.

This new building was put up by Mr Roberts from Bermuda. He came on a visit and applied himself to this task. It was built with burnt brick and cement. It allowed many more procedures to be performed in better conditions. It also allowed reorganisation of the other wards in the hospital and left more space for an administration block.

In October 1983 Cathie was in Lusaka to receive her investiture at State House. Dr Kenneth Kaunda, the president of Zambia, conferred upon her "The Grand Officer of the Eagle of Zambia". This gave the right to use the initials GOEZ after her name. At this time Noeline had retired from hospital work and Cathie was hospital supervisor and sister in charge.

The work at the school was progressing with now nearly 100 children in the school for the physically handicapped. Many of these were taken by Dr Adams to Luanshya for corrective surgery. This was a great blessing to those children and the cost was met by the mine hospital and Mission Medic-air which flew them there and back. One little fellow at the school, Ezekiel, was quite a character. When another boy had stolen his pencil he suggested to the teachers that his punishment should be washing the dishes at the school for one week! Each of these children is different and it was so satisfying to see them develop.

Noeline commenced a book ministry now that she had retired from the hospital. She would go as far Kawama and Chisunka, see the church elders, and sell Bibles and books. Then she visited the prisoners in the jails and left Bible correspondence courses with them. Receiving a quantity of Bemba and English Bibles from the Gideons she distributed them to the guards, prisoners and the police. On the journey home she would call at two villages and give out literature. She also commenced two midweek "Sunday Schools" in nearby villages which around 100 children attended weekly.

Shirley Thomson joined the work in 1984, and she and Mark Davies got married in 1986. During these days Mark continued with his language study and was becoming more fluent in speaking Bemba. In preparation for his marriage he designed and built a fine new house using kiln fired bricks and cement, and metal roofing, with electricity and running water also installed.

Mark was now able to preach a little in Bemba. This was a great help in the churches. Two problems had come to light at a recent conference in the village. First there was a misconception of the way of salvation. Many saw it as a mixture of faith and works, which inevitably leads to the lack of assurance of salvation. So it had to be emphasised that a person is saved by faith alone through grace alone. It is the gift of God and it is not of works (Ephesians 2.8-9). Secondly there was minimal effort made to actually read the Bible. This is something that needs to be addressed time and time again. Daily Bible reading plans were produced to give a systematic pattern for reading the Bible each year.

David Salisbury arrived and he and Mark visited ten secondary schools with the 'Jesus' film. There were 850 students at each presentation, and at four of the schools over a hundred made professions of salvation.

Another two ladies joined the work during 1984 and 1985: Anita Crozier and Margaret King both came and stayed for one year. Stuart and Joy Houghton also came for six months to allow Cathie to go home for a much needed break.

The witchdoctor raised his evil head again and there was another incident of a coffin moving on its own. It fell and got smashed and a new one had to be made. The police came and buried the body, and arrested the two bearers and the two responsible for the person's death. The saddest thing about it was that the man whose body was in the coffin was a member of the church and had been at the church service the previous week. It was impossible to have a service at the house or at the grave, and this caused great grief among the Christians.

In 1985 another very sad incident occurred at the hospital where a nurse, Chisamba, was accused of killing a child. She was taken over the river to Congo and badly beaten, her hair was shaved off, cuts made on her forehead, made to drink village medicine, and kept as a prisoner. At the end of the week she was released and returned to Mambilima. Weaken and bruised it took some weeks for her to be healed but eventually she did and returned to duty.

Henry Pandawe, the son of one of the evangelists, had been educated at the mission school to the level of grade 6. Further education was not possible for lack of funds and his father asked if he could be employed at the hospital as an orderly. He proved himself to be a willing learner and eventually he retired at the age of 60 years having taken over responsibility for the work of the laboratory. He lives in the village at the present day.

Charles Muyembe was brought up at the boarding school. His father was one of the elders in the village. Charles developed a good grasp of the English language and for many years has been a wise elder in the church at Mambilima. He is a good teacher of the Scriptures and till this day he is involved in the work of the Bible school.

Another boy who came through the school was Bwanga Jackson. He also had reached grade 6 but could not go any further with his education. He was employed in the ticket office at the hospital and gradually became involved in work in the wards. Andy Patching taught him basic dentistry during his visits to Mambilima and he became quite proficient in this field. He continued at the hospital until he retired.

Female orderlies were also introduced at this time and they became efficient and proficient members of staff. Included in this group were Miriam, Mary, Lizzie and Phyllis. Then there was Eunice who as a child was very ill but recovered well. As a young adult she worked at the hospital and soon became a reliable worker in the maternity ward. Mary Mwansa was another person who was a great help in this department. She was a rather fat but jolly lady who gave great support to Cathie during these years.

Dr Martin and Mrs Naomi Cooper arrived at Mambilima in 1987. At first they shared a house with Noeline Stockdale. Their luggage had not arrived, so their two boys were without toys for some time. Water and electricity was erratic, and they did not have any form of transport. As a family they had frequent bouts of malaria which weakened them - a good introduction to missionary life! However they settled into the work and eventually began the important task of learning the language.

The arrival of the Coopers was followed by Mr and Mrs Ken Hatcher from Motherwell in 1989 who continued until they retired in 1995. They used their joint experience in administration, nursing and teaching to benefit all of the work at Mambilima. Later that year Mr and Mrs Rod Boatman joined the staff and would be involved in maintenance and building work, and in nursing and midwifery. They continued until in 1991 they moved to Kitwe to continue their service for the Lord.

CHAPTER 17

Changes and Progress

There was much excitement when it was announced that Betty Lammond and Meryl Shepherd were to receive the awards of MBE. Betty and Meryl requested that the awards be presented to them at Mambilima rather than in London or Lusaka. This was kindly accepted by the authorities, and Mr Terry Byrne the British Deputy High Commissioner presented them with their awards in February 1991.

Betty and Meryl's niece Joy came out from the UK for the ceremony and I am grateful to her for recording the details of it. In the days leading up to the ceremony everyone had their tasks to do. Joy was assigned to preparing a photographic display. The school children learned their songs and at the last minute food was prepared. Then she saw bucketfuls of a wobbly substance - it was jelly for the children. They also had ice cream – children's tastes are the same everywhere!

All the congregation was in place and seated, then the long wait began. The children were patient but the roads were bad because of the rains so that the Deputy High Commissioner and his party were late in arriving. Eventually they came! It was strange to see a car flying the Union Jack! The children sang the welcome song and the ceremony began.

Joy noted that all the speakers in the list were noticeably men, celebrating the achievements of two women! "Maybe the choice would be different today," she remarks!

Mr Ken Hatcher chaired the proceedings, and Ba Saute Chikoyi, the first Zambian headmaster gave an introductory speech. Jim Kennedy spoke of the reasons why Betty and Meryl had gone to Mambilima. It was he said, "In obedience to the command of God, in the service of God, and in response to the love of God which they had been shown and to show that love to others."

Meryl Shepherd and Betty Lammond receiving MBE awards, 1991

Then Mr Terry Byrne presented the MBE awards to Betty and Meryl. He gave them a special message from Her Majesty the Queen who said they were "trusty and well loved". Ba Makwaya gave a vote of thanks on behalf of the staff and pupils of Mambilima School. He thanked Mr Byrne for making the long journey, then thanked the two beloved sisters for the work done at the school. Even Queen Elizabeth knew about this school! Then he thanked the missionaries too numerous to name, all the overseas agencies and Mission Medic-Air for their great help. He finished by saying, "May our God and Father Himself and our Lord Jesus Christ be with you who are with us tonight and listen to the beautiful songs of the mosquitoes which are a threat to most Europeans"!!

Mr Chaiwa, a church elder, then closed the proceedings with prayer, and the school choir sang again with great gusto and melody. This was followed by a lovely time wandering around the school taking photos prior to eating a good meal together. Sitting round the table enjoying the food were sixteen adults and three children. It is so good to have times of celebration and rejoicing in life. It compensates for the difficult times! God is good!

Developments at the hospital

During these days of celebration Joy Pope was able to give some assistance in the hospital as a doctor. The help of Fiona Moffat and Anne Hutton, two keen young physiotherapists, was also appreciated as they helped the children through physiotherapy. They also showed the staff how to guide and handle the children to get the best movements for them.

In 1988 Cathie Arthur retired from running the hospital and became involved in visitation work and giving material help in the surrounding villages. Martin Cooper who had been a GP in London took over the administration of the hospital in addition to providing medical care for the patients, with the emphasis on training others. He records how God sent other key staff during his stay. As noted above, Ken Hatcher was involved part time in administration, while Margaret, Ken's wife, worked as a nurse/midwife/tutor and helped part time with the purchase of food and linen. Also Rod Boatman supervised site and vehicle management, and Marja his wife gave great help as a nurse/midwife at the hospital.

Rogers Chama, a social worker, came in 1990 and set up an HIV/AIDS counselling service. The terrible scourge of this disease was now running rampant throughout Central Africa. This talented young man was an able teacher of the Scriptures and helped many to come to faith in Christ. He counselled and advised clients how to cope with their illness and also prepare for death.

Joshua Chama was a boy brought up in the village who went to Lusaka for work, then he returned to Mambilima as a young man and showed great potential. He was appointed as the first hospital administrator and stores manager. Phanuel Tentani came to the hospital in 1993 and was appointed as hospital chaplain to visit patients in their need. He assisted in the counselling of HIV / AIDS patients and also in the management of the hospital.

In 1991 a Hospital Management Team was set up. This was an important step in transferring the running of the hospital from expatriate missionaries to a Zambian missionary board. Martin Cooper considered that this was the most crucial event of this period, allowing the hospital to expand and continue without foreign missionaries.

Cholera struck the village again in 1991 and it was a terrifying experience. Victims of the disease have no control of their bodily functions and become dehydrated very quickly. At this time Margaret Jarvis, Shena McCall and Linley Taylor came through the village as they were fleeing from Luanza on their passage to the Copperbelt. The dreadful smell could be felt as they drew near the hospital. They were exhausted with the journey, and the staff at the hospital were at the end of their tethers with overwork and tiredness. Intravenous fluids were being poured into the patients until the fluids were finished. Water was boiled by the gallon, cooled and given to the patients to drink. The effluent flowed out of the ward and the disinfectants ran dry. It was serious. Thankfully the government cholera team arrived with all the needed supplies and took over the situation giving the nurses a much needed break! Martin records how they saw God provide in so many ways. They used 1,700 litres of IV fluids. They had 256 patients and only 22 had died. Thankfully the outbreak stopped - there were no more IV fluids available in the country.

Ken took over more of the administration of the hospital and was able to organise a government scheme for the Mission to buy mealie-meal. Ken wrote about the many different extra jobs he had to do - such as weighing out food and supervising a small garden. "What do I know about growing rape?" he asked. But his work was of great benefit to all. He took over responsibility for the staff wages and paying accounts, also preparing job descriptions, appointment letters and conditions of service documents. This took a big load away from the doctor to allow his time to be better spent.

Margaret Hatcher too took on more responsibility in the hospital especially when the Coopers were on holiday. When Marja Boatman arrived, she took over in full time hospital/nursing duties and Margaret relieved her on her days off duty. Collation of statistics for the government now was very time consuming

Malaria was still the biggest killer, but HIV/AIDS was catching up. There was such ignorance of the cause of the disease. The government started to advertise the dangers and give advice on how to prevent the disease. However this was not always successful as the disease spread through widespread promiscuity, and the main method of control by using condoms encouraged this. There was a lot more education needed. The answer lies in the biblical message which Christians promote of one marriage partner for life – if only it is heeded. The daily message from the Bible broadcast in the hospital was much needed to help to bring about improvements.

In 1994 the Boatmans left for Europe and did not return to Mambilima but eventually relocated to Kitwe. Ken and Margaret Hatcher spent much time with Joshua Chama and Leonard Mutuka. These were the key men on the Boards of Management and were encouraged to take on responsibility for staff and finance. This was preparing them to take over the running of the hospital and the school.

In 1995 Cathie returned from furlough and was a great help to

125

Ken and Margaret, who spoke very highly of her friendship with Cathie and the care she gave through her now frequent attacks of malaria. Meryl was also a great support and in 1995 Margaret was privileged to take Meryl home to the UK when she completed her service for the Lord in Zambia.

Ken and Margaret returned to the UK for good in 1996. From the UK, Margaret, along with Ian Burness of Echoes of Service, continued to look after the finances for Mambilima. Cathie Arthur retired to Scotland in 1997.

Developments at the school
During these days the Mambilima School for the Physically Handicapped was also progressing. A large block consisting of two dormitories was built for the girls. These included bathing facilities with toilets outside.

Betty and Meryl returned at the end of November 1988 and became totally responsible for the running of the school, and were also involved in much of the teaching. In 1989 Meryl went to the UK to have a knee replacement, leaving Betty with all the responsibility. Meryl returned later that year to continue her duties.

Martin and Naomi Cooper had arrived in 1987. In the UK Naomi had been Deputy Head of a school with disabled children. God had prepared her for the new role she now took up at Mambilima. In January 1991 they took their boys, Jonathan and Ian, to Sakeji School, 1300 miles away in the north west province of Zambia. Naomi recorded that this was the hardest thing she ever had to do in her life. To leave one's own young children at a boarding school can be heart breaking.

Naomi eventually took over the running of the school and relieved both Betty and Meryl. As she became more involved she discovered many things were going missing, and the finger of suspicion pointed at a senior person. When he was removed from the school it became a happier place. Unfortunately this case went to court over a period of a year. During these days the offender was allowed to preach in the church. And at the end of the day the man was pronounced innocent!

It was great to have had Sonny and Marion Roberts from Bermuda visit for six months. They became involved in supervising the building of the children's block and other renovations. Phil Ravesteyn, an Australian with Mobile Mission Maintenance came for two months to supervise building work while Mark Davies was in the UK. He finished the extension to Cathie's house and the dining room for the school.

Daniel Hendricksen came for a gap year between school and university. He helped at the hospital and completed a playground for the children. It was good for the pupils to have a younger lad around. Daniel was a big asset to the team and the many jobs he did relieved the pressure on other staff.

Martin and Naomi suffered from many bouts of malaria, some very severe requiring treatment by intravenous infusion. One such episode occurred when Naomi's parents were with them. However they were grateful for her dad creating a programme on the computer for the staff wages, which made things much easier.

There was one boy in the school who was very badly handicapped. His name was John. He had been born a normal child but had taken ill when he was two years of age. He was taken to the nearest health facility but no tests were performed, and chloroquine was injected into his body. The death sentence to his lower limbs was pronounced. He suffered from poliomyelitis from that day on.

His future from then on was very insecure. The problems of life became insurmountable. Education was extremely inaccessible to persons with physical limitations, and a job opportunity was a farfetched pipe dream.

Harvest time for him was always a time of rejoicing and for a spell gave relief from toil. This was especially so when there was a bumper crop and the barns were full. Full stomachs also eased the burdens of life. Social gatherings in the evenings continued into the night and were an outpost of mischief for boys. They were soothing periods after the business of the day.

John was brought up in an era of strong superstitions coupled with hard to believe traditional concepts. When ordinary health services failed to help, suffering people blamed one another for practising witchcraft.

John's formal education started at home where he began to read both the English and Bemba languages and became fluent in both. As a result he began school in grade 3 at Mambilima. The two "white missionary ladies" took great care of him and guided him in his future development.

He was a bright student, and gained a place at St Clements Secondary School. This school of excellence had students from a diverse spread of social classes. They were meant to live as equals but John records "this was as unworkable as mixing sugar and salt to make a tasty cup of tea". He had great problems because of his physical handicap, but by the help of the Lord and good hard work he endured and was successful.

After completion of his higher education John applied for a post as a teacher at Mambilima School. His inability to take physical education classes caused a bit of a problem. However the school board met to discuss his case. Some of the missionaries argued his case coherently saying someone like this would be an inspiration to the students. Eventually in 1990 he was accepted as a teacher and joined the staff where he still continues to great effect.

There were other more serious problems among the staff at this time. These included constitutional issues with regard to the church affiliation of the Head Teacher. At one stage the Head was a member of the Jehovah's Witnesses. Since the school was a CMML school, the person leading the school must be prepared to uphold the beliefs of CMML. These matters were discussed and eventually a proper constitution was agreed and put in place.

Mr Leonard Mutuka took over as Deputy Head, and in 1993 the Coopers finally left Mambilima. Martin had a relapse of his TB and was very ill, so much so that Naomi's parents came and helped them to pack up their goods. They collected their boys from Sakeji School and returned to the UK.

So we reach another milestone in the long story of Mambilima mission. The workers come and go, there is constant change, but the work goes on. In His great goodness God is with His servants all the days of their lives while they go on following Him.

CHAPTER 18

New Opportunities in the 90s

Now that Marja Boatman was working in the hospital, Margaret Hatcher had a wonderful opportunity to teach Religious Education in the Government School. The opening came at Mulundu School, the one which was in the village. Facilities were few but it was a privilege to teach two classes of 14 to 17 year olds with forty students in each class.

R E was taught according to the government curriculum featuring the Christian faith equally with other faiths, but not failing to speak forcibly about the inerrant Word of God. The two classes became four as time went by. Margaret was able to present the Christian point of view and to commend the gospel and the Bible in almost every lesson. The exam results were very good.

Ken and Margaret were asked to lead a Bible study in English for teachers and others who were interested. This took place in their home every Friday and also there was a Bible study for staff on a Wednesday afternoon when the emphasis was on its practical application to daily living. This continued throughout the years. They also had a lifelong interest and involvement in Scripture Union and this was another ongoing work in the schools. Both were involved in running the Scripture Union classes at Mulundu School using Bibles and chorus books which they supplied, and they had a great time with the students.

As the years progressed Saturday rallies were introduced with as many as 50 to160 attending from 7am till 4pm. There was great singing, prayers and Bible lessons, with Bible quizzes and activity worksheets being introduced. One of the vital parts of such rallies was the food - both breakfast and a main meal were provided. Cathie, Margaret and the Zambian sisters enjoyed these times enormously.

Literature work was now becoming a major feature of the work at Mambilima. Large quantities of Bibles and books were being sold from a very cramped shop and storeroom. Ken Hatcher and Mark Davies had a vision to increase the literature work. So after prayer, and discussion with other leaders they decided to build a Christian Centre. This would include a bookshop, a store and a reading room that could be used to develop the Emmaus work and other evangelical outreach.

Mark supervised the building and it was a great day in March 1991 when the new "Kabelenga Christian Centre" was opened. Over 500 Christians from the surrounding area attended the opening at which Mr Jim Kennedy gave the message and the blessing. Mark and Shirley Davies moved to Samfya in 1991 having made such an important contribution to the work at Mambilima. They agreed to continue supervising the literature work and they visited regularly.

On the 31st October 1991 there was a General Election in Zambia. This ended the term of office of Dr Kenneth Kaunda who was the first elected President. The new president was Frederick Chiluba, a man from the Luapula who had attended school at Mambilima. He was a Christian, and in a speech shortly after his appointment he commended both Cathie and Margaret for their work and commitment to the Zambian people.

After Ken and Margaret returned from furlough in December 1991, they were led to take up the work of running the new Christian Centre. Bibles, books, Emmaus courses, stationery and other essential sundries were sold. A Zambian lad was in charge of the bookshop. A lending library and a reading room were staffed by volunteers and were well used. Seminars on various topics were introduced, including Sunday School teacher training, caring for new converts, how to study the Bible, and basic homiletics for choir leaders and others.

Cathie and Margaret used the reading room weekly for a class of 22 young Zambian ladies to teach the basic skills of sewing. Some learned how to use an electric sewing machine and made their own clothes. They enjoyed singing the choruses and the short epilogue.

Mission workers who had some ability to preach were more involved in telling of the Saviour. Most CMML churches had two services each Sunday and these brothers were used widely in these services. Ken travelled from church to church around the area giving great help. He felt it a priority to teach the children and he would make sure he was there early in the morning for the Sunday School. This often meant him leaving the previous day to get to a distant church. He was able to preach in Bemba but this took a lot of preparation on his part. He reached as far north as Kawambwa, and visited many large boarding schools where he sold Bibles to the pupils and staff, and had many encouraging conversations.

Mambilima has always been a place that many visitors came to. These included Peter Grosvenor, Ian Burness, and Mr and Mrs Stan Warren from Echoes of Service, also Jim and Ruth McLellan and Jim and Margaret Hopewell from Interlink, a group from Bermuda, and other missionaries from time to time over many years as the visitors book can testify.

Thus the Word of God continued to be brought to young and old. Many trusted the Saviour, were baptised, and added to the local churches in the area. The period of having foreign missionaries was coming to a close, but the work was moving forward in the hands of Zambian believers.

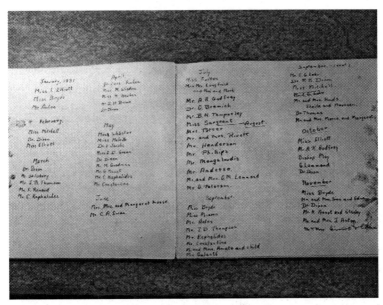

Visitors' Book for Mambilima, 1931

CHAPTER 19

Robert's First Impressions

My first introduction to Mambilima was in early 1997 when we passed through the Mission while evacuating from danger in the Democratic Republic of Congo. We did not linger because we were eager to get to the Copperbelt to let our relatives know that we were safe. Just a quick meal and we were on our way.

We spent some time going from pillar to post on the Copperbelt before collecting our new Landrover from South Africa, then we settled with Ray and Terry Barham in Mansa for a few months for me to try and learn the language.

At this time plans were being made for the centenary of the first CMML work in Zambia - at Mambilima. Scott and Holly Kitchen who were resident at Mambilima had gone home to the USA and as it was doubtful if they would return. Margaret and I were asked if we would go to Mambilima and act as hosts to the visitors coming to the celebrations. So this is what we did.

Initially we took up residence in the house known as Cathie Arthur's house. The house was in the same condition as she had left it in 1997. The first memorable impression I had was the smell in the house! It was a new smell to me – it really stank! It invaded the whole house and pervaded everything. It was caused by the large amount of bats living in the roof space.

The living room was completely furnished with a beautiful table and comfortable chairs. The kitchen had a cooker and a supply of water. The bath was solid, made of cast iron, and very deep. How it had been transported from South Africa was a mystery. Unfortunately the water supply to it was not working. To have a bath the procedure was to add one bucket of boiling water to two of cold. The temperature was just right but the depth minimal!

Attached to this house was the extension Ken and Margaret Hatcher had built. It had its own facilities with two large bedrooms upstairs. There was a secondary lighting system installed, operated from a large battery. An emergency alarm system worked off the battery, sounding a horn to alert people to any danger.

Before the celebrations Margaret and I moved into the house that the Kitchens had vacated since they were not returning. This was the house built by Mark Davies for his bride Shirley. It was built with kiln fired brick and cement and is a substantial building. We have occupied this house until the present time and find it very comfortable.

On settling into Mambilima we soon became aware of many areas in which we could be involved. The hospital required help, and as we were both nurses we could assist there, particularly in administration. We were also teachers and could give some assistance in the school. We saw that little had been done on building maintenance at both hospital and school since the missionaries had left. It was obvious that there was plenty of work available to keep us busy. There was also an evident need for preaching and teaching the Word of God.

Soon after we settled the church elders from the district met with us. They discussed how they saw us being able to help in the spiritual work in the area. They said that there were many evangelists that went out into the villages and preached the Good News. But there was a definite need for Bible teaching and we discussed how we could help. Another needy area was the supply of Bibles and good literature for Christians to read, both in Bemba and in English. It appeared to us that there were going to be endless opportunities for us to use our God given abilities.

We were invited to join the Hospital and School Boards of Management, and this we did. These were interesting times as we sat round the table to discuss the business. I found the proceedings very pedantic and laborious – I had to get used to the cultural differences. I was also amazed at how little money was available to run the two establishments. They really were operating on a shoe string budget! Our learning was on a very steep upward curve.

Money for the Hospital came from a variety of sources. The Government supplied some via the District Management Team; some staff were paid via the Churches Medical Association of Zambia; Echoes of Service gifted money from overseas. Margaret and I would now be responsible for handling this gift money from UK. We had to evaluate the way this was used and make some adjustments to accountability.

The hospital was situated in the centre of the Mission and all the villagers just walked through the grounds. There was little or no security. We discovered that many items went missing from the wards. Sheets, mattresses and medicines were all being stolen. Margaret spent many hours investigating this and unearthing huge discrepancies. Eventually this led to resignations and dismissals from the administrator down.

Surveying the buildings at the hospital showed a great need to upgrade or renew some of them. Money was negotiated to erect a concrete wall fence around the hospital to give some security. Contracts were arranged to make the concrete blocks, builders were hired and the building work commenced.

During these early days news came to the Administrator that a doctor was coming to Mambilima. Said he, "Better hurry and get the mortuary ready since a doctor is coming"! The doctor who came was from VSO (Voluntary Service Overseas). Her name was Dr Sue Levy, a converted Jew from the south of England.

These were still difficult and turbulent days. Medicines were still going missing from the hospital. Vital drugs to treat patients were not to be found. But anyone could go to one of the stores in the village and buy any drug you wanted, and all supplied in a Government of Zambia bag! Now where did they get them from?

Dr Sue did not speak Bemba and required a nurse with her to interpret for the patients. She was a very capable lady who was most caring of her patients. However the staff thought they would exert some control over her movements. This situation had to be dealt with quickly, and we were grateful for the services of the District Nursing Officer who quenched this rebellion by the staff!

Dr Sue was her own person and quite a character. Well we remember the first time she suffered from an attack of malaria. Margaret and I were returning from a preaching trip. We were stopped near the village and told to get back quickly as the doctor was sick. Well, Sue was ill with a high temperature, and dehydrating from vomiting.

"Is there room in your freezer, Margaret," she said. "Why?" Margaret asked. "I'm dying and I don't want to be buried in Africa, take my body to England" she said! Margaret took over and intramuscular quinine was prescribed. "Not such a large needle," she cried. "I'm in charge!" was the reply, and into her buttock it sank! Dr Sue recovered but it took a long time to clear and she had a relapse on returning to England.

It was during these days that a visit was made to the mission by a young, bright academic who was doing some research into how the early missionaries did their work. It struck me that she already had her conclusions in mind before she started the research. Her view was that the missionaries wrote letters home telling of all the great things they were doing to make them look big and important; that the treatment they meted out was for their own benefit more than that of the patients.

Some of the older mission workers were interviewed in her study. Questions were asked via an interpreter, Margaret helped with some of these. One who was questioned was old Yotam, an ex laundry worker.

"Tell me," she asked, "what did Mr Lammond do?"

"He sawed off patient's legs," he replied.

"Did he ask the patient if he could saw off their leg," she asked.

"Of course!" he said.

"Why did he saw off the leg?"

"Because of the deep sores which would not heal."

"Did they object to having their leg sawed off?"

"They would have been daft to object, they were going to die," he said, and muttered under his breath about the wisdom of this woman.

Another old worker from the hospital was asked about Miss Stockdale.

"Did Miss Stockdale ever get annoyed and angry?" he was asked.

"Never," was the reply.

"Are you saying that she never lost her temper?"

"Never!" he replied, and refused to be involved any further.

Great to see the loyalty of the staff to the missionaries!

Margaret asked if she could see the study when it was finished. "You missionaries will never want to read this when it is finished," she answered. That day I learned how not to do research. We never heard another word from her!

This was how our experience with God began among the people of Mambilima and the Luapula.

CHAPTER 20

The Centenary Conference, 1998

This was a momentous occasion in the history of the CMML churches in Zambia. It was 100 years since the gospel of Christ first arrived in the country. As we have been recording the history of these years, great changes had taken place. Now there were thousands of followers of the Lord Jesus Christ. This celebration would above all be to glorify God.

The excitement grew in the village and throughout the valley as the time of this conference drew near. August arrived before we knew it! A site for the conference was chosen down by the river. Here there were massive rock formations made by what looked like small stones being fused together by a great heat. A prominent feature was a huge elevated rock with a large overhang resting on a small base, which it was decided to use for the pulpit. The preaching desk was under the overhang and upon the stony outcrop below. Farther down was the area where the choirs would gather to sing their songs.

The rock provided shade from the burning heat of the sun, and underneath the foundation was firm. The congregation sat in a large semi circle all round the rock pulpit. Eventually wooden poles were cemented into the ground and reed mats laid over these to protect the audiences from the sun. It was, and is, an idyllic place with a view extending over the beautiful Luapula River to the Democratic Republic of Congo on the other side. In addition the site was very biblical - we have been taken from a horrible pit and our feet placed upon a rock (Psalm 40.2), and truly we were under the shadow of a great rock in a weary land (Isaiah 32.2)!

Across the large site areas were set aside for living accommodation, pits were dug and latrines erected. Wood was cut and carried for cooking food. Water was brought from the river. The people would build vertical shelters for their living quarters – roofs were not needed as it would not rain! Separate bathing areas were set aside at the river for men and women. Dangerous parts of the river where a crocodile might loiter were avoided!

Three Boys on a Safe Seat, 2002

At the mission as well it was all go. Rooms were being prepared, extra beds put in place and made ready. Some would need to sleep in tents, and where would they wash? How would we be able to feed all our visitors? Food was bought in and frozen or stored in the pantry.

Suddenly the time was upon us! A small plane was heard buzzing overhead. It soon landed at the airstrip bringing in some of the overseas visitors. Others came by car, or truck, or canoe. What a sight it was also to see large numbers of families arriving on foot or on bicycle, with goods and chattels for a week of camping. Soon there were 10,000 people getting themselves into the camping area.

The many oversees visitors included Dr Ian Burness from Echoes of Service, Jim and Ruth McLellan from Interlink, Mr William Yuille from CMML Canada (all were Scots), Mr Bruce Poidevin from CMML Flight Service, Cathie Arthur, Alan and Sheila Park and family, Ray and Terry Barham, Ruth Gray, Mark Davies (nearly all Scots), Margaret Brown, Dorothy Collins from New Zealand, and Linda Beer.

Then the singing commenced and the air was filled with praise and rejoicing for God's unfailing goodness over these one hundred years. Prayer, praise and thanksgiving was made to the Lord over and over again. It was truly a wonderful time.

The day of the actual celebration arrived, and the Government Minister of Religion swept into the site in his car along with his retinue. He was representing President Chiluba who was unable to come. This was a disappointment since he had attended the school at Mambilima. But the Minister was an exceptionally nice man, a lovely Christian who gave a powerful word of encouragement.

The visitors who came from overseas were from Scotland, England, Canada and USA. All had some input into the conference. Papers were presented on the various aspects of the work in Zambia and how it began in the Luapula Province. Those involved in the presentation of papers were Ray Barham, Mark Davies, Jellicoe Mumba and Kovina Mutenda.

Lunch time arrived and the house was full to overflowing. Over thirty people were fed that day inside the house, and many more belonging to the army and the police force outside. How it was done I do not know, but food appeared and was eaten - and yes, there was plenty left over. It was not quite the feeding of the 5,000, but it did seem an awful lot of people! Our God is still able to perform miracles.

The celebrations went on for some time as day after day there were services morning, afternoon and evening. It was a great time of rejoicing and also much blessing when many people trusted the Lord Jesus as their Saviour.

But sadly everything must come to an end! However a picnic lunch was organised for the last day before we dispersed from each other. A beautiful site was chosen for this on a safe river with beautiful waterfalls. Some enjoyed the relaxation and others went swimming, followed by a really enjoyable lunch. Then we all went off in various directions, back to the routine of work life. As we looked back on 100 years of the goodness of God we have fresh cause to trust Him as we go forward - until the Lord returns again as He has promised to do.

At the centenary meeting it was announced that President Chiluba had donated the conference site as a present to CMML, and he also gave a monetary gift to help develop the site. A committee was set up to administer this gift and they chose to build a concrete wall around the site. Eventually this was completed to mark the boundary, and an entrance gate was installed.

This site was now going to be used only once every second year for the provincial conference when thousands would gather from all over Zambia. But the amenities were very limited, and Margaret and I had a vision to see this developed further as a camp centre. So in 2008 two blocks of ten rooms were built, one for men and the other for women. Each was built with kiln fired bricks and cement and a metal roof, with an ablution and a toilet block adjacent. Then a three bedroom house was erected for a caretaker and his family. In 2010 two 1000 litre water tanks were installed, filled by a pump in the river, to give a water supply to the facilities on the site.

The Luapula regional conference is held here every two years in the month of August. This is an event that attracts visitors from all over Zambia and Congo. It lasts for one week and is a great time of rejoicing. Every time it is held I am reminded of the Feast of Tabernacles where the people of Israel lived in booths and every day they rejoiced before the Lord. Now approximately 16,000 attend over the week and it is a moving sight to behold.

The camp is wakened at 5am and a morning song of worship is sung over the amplifiers. Prayers are made and the morning routines commence. Before mid-day, two teaching sessions are held, interspersed with many choirs singing their hearts out. In the afternoon there is another teaching session, then two in the evening when the gospel is preached.

Between each session there are great times of fellowship and new friendships are made. Food is cooked on *babulas* all over the camp, the delicious smell of cooking all around wafting towards preachers and listeners as the teaching is given. It can be a big distraction!

The fellowship and rejoicing continues all night until 11pm when the last hymn is sung, and the camp committed in prayer to the Lord for the night. Soon it will be morning and it will start all over again.

The meetings on the Lord's Day are extra special, particularly the time for the Lord's Supper or Communion Service. To sit reverently along with around 8,000 believers and hear one brother after another giving thanks to God for sending His Son to die for our sins, to give to the Lord Jesus the worship and adoration due to Him for His great love - it is so very special and moving.

Now a committee has taken over the running of the site. In addition to the wooden poles to hold shading from the sun, blocks have been made for seating. Although some development has taken place, there is room for much more. We pray for a leader to be raised up by God to see the great potential here for camp work, a person with a vision to take forward the development and see the site used for all types of outreach work. Oh that God would stir up someone to give their life to this work!

Some Scottish Missionaries in Zambia from the late 1900s
From left, Back row:
Cathie Arthur, Alan & Sheila Park, Robert Muir, Ken Hatcher
Front row:
Jean Kruse, May Montgomery, Margaret Hatcher,
Margaret Muir, Jean Jappy

CHAPTER 21

Recent Hospital Developments

When Margaret and I went to Mambilima in 1998 it was obvious to us that we would have a limited span of working life available. Observing how the work had been already Zambianized, we believed that it would soon be totally in Zambian hands. But in the short spell without expatriate mission workers much of the property had deteriorated. I quickly learnt that 'maintenance' was not in the local vocabulary! So we decided that we would build on the good work already done and hope to leave the hospital in as good a condition as possible.

The first task we tackled was the upgrading and painting of the maternity unit. It was 12 years since that had been done and it was really needing to be taken down and replaced. Help was promised from the government but as yet nothing was forthcoming. The big problem is that the government will not officially recognise the hospital for what it is, rather classifying it as a rural health centre.

The government was insisting that the Outpatient Department be separate from the hospital and have its own entrance. A gift was sent from a lady in Scotland, and with this the Murray OPD was built. This had a waiting room, two consulting rooms, a treatment room, a pharmacy and a records office, a very convenient place for staff to work in.

The original hospital building was falling down so it was demolished and also the old OPD. This gave some limited space for an operating theatre. Building this was to be a community project but it did not get beyond the foundations level. After a number of years we decided to take it on. We drew up plans to try to fit all that was needed into the space available, and although not perfect it would be workable.

Contracts for building were drawn up and eventually the building took shape. Furniture was supplied from the Zambian government and some from overseas. Eventually John Moyo, a clinical officer, joined the staff. He had the ability to do some limited surgery. Eventually he took further studies and became a medical licentiate. He was a very capable fellow but at times it was like handling a bucking horse!

Theatre furniture was supplied from a variety of sources - the autoclave (steam sterilizer) from the Netherlands government; the operating table, lamp and anaesthetic machine from Medical International; air conditioning from the Zambian government. It was a great shame that it was so difficult to get gas for the anaesthetic machine!

Then two new wards for women were built. The funding for this came from an old lady in Scotland. Each week she put money aside in a polythene bag and kept it under her bed. I think she denied herself chocolate biscuits to do this! When the bag was full she arranged for the money to be sent to Zambia, and from this the McQueen Women's wards were built.

Next task was to demolish other buildings and build two new wards for men. At the same time a new laboratory was built and extra equipment obtained which was needed as the hospital was now a counselling and treatment centre for HIV/AIDS. Those enlisted on the programme were given free treatment. Such treatment was successful and with it patients can have as much as an extra 15 years of good lifestyle.

Since then progress has continued and regular upgradings made. Air conditioning was put into the theatre and laboratory, and a large diesel generator installed to supply electricity when the power fails (which it often does). Some of the grounds were landscaped and some fruit trees planted.

The old laboratory was converted into offices to give a work area for secretarial support, later computers were installed which assisted with the administration.

A previous consulting area had fallen into disrepair. The lower walls were still standing but all the upper supports had long since gone. Building upon these lower walls, two offices were made and a conference room / board room erected. This too has proved to be a big asset to the site.

A dental suite was added - a rather grandiose name for the building but it had a dental chair and a set of dental forceps! This was put in place for a student who had been sponsored to take a dental course. Unfortunately at the end of the course he refused to return to complete the contracted two years post-course experience! You learn to take the bad with the good!

Malnutrition is still a big problem, especially in children. There was also a need for a high dependency unit for children who have suffered burns. A four bedded room was added to the children's ward and a kitchen installed. Extra heating was installed because children with burns and malnutrition can suffer from hypothermia. The kitchen gave an opportunity to teach cooking and feeding skills to parents.

Patients come to the hospital from a wide area, and their relatives also come to help in their care. The accommodation for all who were coming was inadequate. In 2008 a block of 10 rooms was added where the relatives could sleep and cook their food. Added to this were toilet and washing facilities.

Waste disposal in a rural area is always a problem. There is no 'refuse collection' and digging a big hole is not always the best way to dispose of things. An incinerator was built in the grounds which fulfilled government standards and this has met a real need. As toilets are of the "long drop" variety - they need to be replaced from time to time.

In 2009 the government was responsible for building a house for a doctor, and in 2010 it was completed and occupied. Also at the same time a grant was received from the Beit Trust to build another three houses. The hospital now has a supply of good, well constructed houses with electricity, water on tap, flushing toilets and bathing facilities. Many have added satellite television which is seen as a big bonus when working in a rural setting.

All these facilities are for the benefit of the patients. They are fed twice daily with a basic diet cooked on the premises on charcoal *babulas*. The cook likes to look the part and wears his chef's hat! But as well as their physical care their spiritual care is very important. The hospital is there to show something of the love of God in a practical fashion. Every morning a service is broadcast over the loudspeakers, with a timely message given by a variety of church members. Patients are visited personally, and counselling and encouragement given. Local church groups visit from time to time and the choirs sing to the patients. Many have had not only healing of the body but also have found salvation for their souls and the real meaning of life through trusting Jesus Christ.

At the time of our arrival in 1998 Joshua Chama was the Administrator, Kaoma Nsabaula was the accountant, and Sue Levy the doctor. In many ways this was an unhappy time and Sue found it difficult because of the attitude of staff towards her. Eventually she had to return to England because of her mother's illness. Then Joshua Chama resigned from his post, and his deputy Phanuel Tentani Mwaba, who was also the HIV/Aids counsellor, was appointed as Administrator.

Kaoma Nsabaula and Tentani Mwaba, 2009

We had the joy of encouraging Tentani in this new role. We saw his abilities develop as he returned from a variety of courses. His style was slow and pedantic but he was thorough and dependable. For Margaret and myself he became a reliable friend who supported us in our days of difficulty and stress. It is with sadness that we have to mention his death even as we write.

Kaoma Nsabaula has worked hard and well as the accountant. He made the change from working a manual system to entering the computer age. This young man has kept pace with progress and it has been a real joy to work with him. Accounts were kept accurately and statements produced exactly on time. He has given loyal service to the hospital and to the Lord in His service, and has been of great support to ourselves.

I must watch how I write now as I am beginning to feel a bit like King David with his lists of mighty men! However these are those who over the years have become very close and dear to us. But there are others who have given much loyal service. Honesty Muyembe worked for many years in the laundry. In these early days the linen had to be carried down to the river and washed by hand, then there was the drying, ironing and repairing. He is an unsung hero! Now there is an automatic washing machine to do all the work!

Other loyal workers who have given sterling and dependable service over many years include the following: Muke Emmanuel skilfully operated the X-ray equipment; Saikalo Cibesa was a support worker who did a pharmacy course and is now the qualified pharmacist; also Kapya, Ivy, Josephine and Mofia, all helpful characters with their own individual personalities.

More recently other developments have made a big improvement in the hospital facilities. The Lord has supplied many goods from the UK via the good services of Medical Missionary News. The latest load (2010 and 2011) was a supply of 62 adjustable height beds which came from two hospitals in Scotland where wards were being closed so that the beds were surplus to requirements. Power cleaned and sanitised they were loaded into a container along with as many bedside lockers for patients. New mattresses were made and bought in Zambia and the beds covered with new white sheets. Delighted staff said with glee, "We are now the London hospital!"

Patient transport has always been a big problem. Back in 2000 a second-hand fully fitted ambulance was bought which gave good service. Later the government provided a completely new one. But keeping vehicles in good condition is difficult - roads are not good and tyres do not last very long. Dennis the driver tries to maintain the vehicles in good order but it is a big job.

The government has now made plans to upgrade the place and give it full hospital status. But we have found that the fulfilment of plans is a slow business – they change frequently! However, over the years God has used the hospital to bless thousands of people with a "healing of body and of soul" experience. New life has come into the world here as babies are born, and eternal life has been found by many as they are born again. God is being glorified and men and women are being blessed.

Outpatient Clinic, 1980

Waiting Area, 1990

Building Theatre, 2005

McQueen Women's Ward, 2006

CHAPTER 22

Mambilima School in the 21st Century

This residential school took only physically handicapped children when we arrived. There were classes from grades 1 – 7 with girls and boys of a variety of ages. The girls lived in two large dormitories, and the bigger boys in a variety of rooms at the other end of the school. The younger boys were accommodated in two dormitories in the centre of the premises. Here again we could see deterioration in the buildings due to lack of maintenance as we could work out from photos from earlier days.

In Zambian rural culture it is difficult for physically handicapped and deformed children to be accepted in society. Many believe that their situation is the result of witchcraft and will avoid being near the children. So they would not be welcome in an ordinary school, and besides this the facilities at such schools would not be suitable for many such children.

We began negotiations with the education authorities to extend the school to enable the children to continue their education to grades 8 and 9. Permission was granted, but for this to happen more classrooms were required. The original building opened in 1931 by Mr Swan was showing signs of its age, so it was decided to go for a new purpose built school with appropriate facilities for handicapped children.

Brass Tacks (British Assemblies Tactical Support) were contacted, and they agreed to help. Plans were drawn up, approved, and dates of commencement agreed. Colin Breeze and a team of five workers from the UK came out to Mambilima in April 2004. Contracts were arranged with local builders, carpenter, electrician and labourers to assist in the work. Soon work commenced, starting each day at daybreak before the sun was high and finished in the early afternoon. Breakfast and a main meal were supplied for all the workers, giving work for a number of ladies from the church.

This was a real happy time as those from overseas laboured hard along with the local men. Often we saw how the Lord would supply our need just in the nick of time. When power was needed to work the tools, the Zambian electricity board supplied it within just 24 hours, something unheard of before. When the mission truck gave up the ghost completely one Saturday and threatened to disrupt the supply mechanism, another small truck which had been purchased six months previously arrived unexpectedly - within two hours! - supplied at the right time by the Lord who knew the need. When food was required to feed hungry men, a supply of dried goods arrived from UK. Cement was delivered on time, special bolts made in a factory in the Copperbelt were delivered by bus. Yes, the Lord gave help and met our every need.

Along with this major project, at the same time the Brass Tacks team extended the school dining room, doubling its size. Trees were removed, foundations dug and the building erected – all without mechanical lifting equipment, only many strong and willing workers!

We now have school buildings that are the strongest and best built in the Luapula valley. They are a credit to the team. As an extra, they laid the foundations for the new church building on their day off!

The Brass Tacks team found relaxation in a variety of ways. After work some hired bicycles and went off into the village, some were taken out fishing in dugout canoes on the river, others enjoyed visiting their new friends in their homes, some bought snakes and skinned them. All went to bed exhausted and slept without rocking!

We did enjoy the help and fellowship of Bert and Isobel Cargill when the team were with us that year. Once on a day off work, as a group we took a trip 100 miles north to Lake Mweru. After enjoying the beauty of the lake, looking round the village and the market, hunger came upon us. We had brought a picnic with us, but one of the village 'restaurants' said they could supply us with chips and eggs - if we bought the potatoes and the eggs for them to cook! We did this but it turned out to be a real fiasco. Only Jim Smith managed to get his chips and eggs before the gas ran out. The rest of us ate our sandwiches!

Working with Brass Tacks was a great learning experience for the local men. They were taught new skills in all aspects of building, and from then on the local men have been able to do more building work to the same high standard.

At the school pupils could now be taken to the level of grades 8 and 9. With the extensions made to both school and hospital a supply of clean water was now needed. A gift from the Guernsey Government was used to sink a borehole in 2006, so now the school and hospital, particularly the operating theatre, all have a supply of clean water. At the same time the old rusting metal water tanks were replaced with large new plastic ones.

As the school expanded more teachers and more housing were required. A new house was built with all facilities by means of another grant from the Beit Trust. This Christian Trust from Zimbabwe has been most supportive of the school and hospital, and we have appreciated the great help Mr David Moffat has given.

Over the years the standard of education has remained high

and the children have achieved a high pass rate in their exams. The teaching of the Scriptures is of prime importance. Bible reading and prayers take place in the dormitories each night. There is Scripture Union and school assembly each week, with Sunday School and the church service attended each Lord's Day. Many children have come to faith in the Lord Jesus while at the school.

Because of their physical disability very few pupils were able to extend their education beyond grade 9. Requests were made that the children who were able should have the opportunity to go to High School, as had been the desire of many for some time. Again negotiations commenced with the education authority for this to come to fruition - they were very supportive and in principle said yes.

This was going to be a major development which would require more classrooms and living accommodation. Plans were made for a block of three classrooms, with offices for teachers and store rooms. In 2009 work commenced using these builders trained by Brass Tacks. Now there is a beautiful building made with kiln fired bricks and cement, faced on the outside and plastered in the inside. There is wheelchair access to all rooms and facilities very suitable for learning.

At the same time as this we changed the use of another building. A strong building had been put up with a view to rearing pigs but unfortunately this pig project was a disaster and did not materialize. However the building was easy to convert into suitable dormitory accommodation. It now houses five dormitory rooms for four boys in each, a large sitting/study room, a flat for a house parent, and toilets and showers. This building is in the area where the school playing ground had once been, which again had fallen into disrepair. The 'stitch in time saves nine' proverb is not known in rural Zambia!

Plans were then made for an accommodation block for girls at the High School. This was modelled on the dormitories at Chengelo School. There are eight rooms for two girls in each, also two blocks with toilets and showers, a flat for a houseparent and a large entrance/sitting room. This was built in 2010 and is a great facility for the High School girls.

William Chibangu was appointed as Head Teacher of the High School. We had watched this young man grow educationally and spiritually, and were able to help him develop in his life, a very capable and steady person whom we could trust. He became an elder in the church and was involved in teaching the scriptures. However, the government also saw his potential and in 2010 promoted him to Inspector of Schools. But in this way God has sent a capable man with his wife and family to another needy part of His harvest field.

The first class in the High School started in 2010. The first places were given to the handicapped children who had achieved the required standard. After this a few places were available for children from the local village to join the class. These children are not in residence. These pupils are now in grade 12 and will complete their education this year, with a grade 10 and 11 following on behind them.

The High School has now been fully gazetted (officially recognised) and is known as Mambilima High School. As usual some more adjustments have had to be made. The building opened in 1931 is being used as a science lab at present, but foundations have been laid for a completely new laboratory supplied by the government. This will mature in the fullness of time!

Over these last 14 years there have been times of great difficulty with staff, as well as joyous days. When we arrived Mr Matuka was head teacher. He was a real friend, with a great knowledge of the Bible. He acted as my interpreter on many occasions and could be saying it in Bemba as I was saying it in English! He died as a young man.

Mr Milner Lubumbe, his deputy, was then appointed head. He had a lovely wife and family and we were very friendly. Unfortunately he became over friendly with one of the female teachers. This quickly became known by the pupils. His marriage broke up and his family divided. The school children were being beaten because they told others about what was happening. We had the heartache of trying to deal with this situation, spending many hours counselling and trying to rescue it. Then there was the disciplinary hearing with the school board and the removal of the offender from the school. All this affected Margaret and me more than we can tell.

The Board of Management then appointed Mr Mwewa Kayabala as Head Teacher. He was a Mambilima man, well educated, and an elder in the local church. The school moved forward under his leadership, and he was with us often and interpreted for me and other preachers on many occasions. Then problems began to arise with lack of accountability with regard to finance. Many questions were being asked regarding lack of payments to suppliers of goods to the school. This led further to unacceptable irregularities involving pupils in the school.

Again we were in the sad situation of investigation and discipline, with hours of precious time spent on these matters. At such times your soul is not at rest and it affects your ability to be free and fluent in studying and teaching the scriptures. God's people are not getting the best they deserve. But we do praise God that we can say with another "He gives His beloved sleep" and each night as we lay down we were given the most refreshing sleep.

Mr Kayabala had to leave the school and the house where he lived which was next to ours. At this time his dear wife was very sick and now the whole family has been affected. Such problems cause upset in the churches and in the villages. It is so sad to see those you have trusted fall into the temptation of either Sex or Silver or Self Pride, and sometimes all three!

The new Head appointed by the school Board of Management was Mr Musukambale, an elder from another church along the valley. He was with us for only a short time, however, before he was promoted to the big government school in the village. Such movement of senior staff is unsettling to everyone, but the work still goes forward.

Over the years there has been a very useful and productive exchange link with the pupils of Chengelo School. Chengelo is a large Christian school with pupils drawn from the upper classes of society. For one week per year a group of these pupils come to Mambilima to see how those from a poor background are educated. This is reciprocated when a group from Mambilima visit Chengelo for one week.

Those from Chengelo appear to give away half of their belongings as they return. I don't know what their parents must think! The tales from those returning to Mambilima are interesting. Some said they were allowed to wash in a big pot! - they had been in the swimming pool! It is an entirely different culture and experience for our children. To go canoeing and abseiling for them is to do the impossible! Mr Thomson and his staff at Chengelo are so good with the children.

During these years John Kalaba, a man with severe physical disabilities, has continued as a teacher at the school and has given faithful and loyal service. To help overcome his difficulties an electric scooter was gifted and sent out from Northern Ireland - this has been a real life line for John. In 2010 John was appointed to the post of deputy Head Teacher at the basic school. The children love him as he is able to empathise with their situation.

Thus into a new century the Mambilima schools for the physically handicapped have moved forward. Young men and women are being educated for life in both the spiritual and secular domain. Physically many have been helped by surgery to their limbs. Our great burden now is where do they go after completion of their schooling? So very few of them are able to get jobs because of the situation in the country and because of their limitations. But we cannot fail to give thanks to God for what has been accomplished in His Name.

School Children after Corrective Surgery, 2009

CHAPTER 23

Bible Teaching 1998 - 2012

Discussion with the elders soon after we arrived at Mambilima showed that there was a great need for Bible teaching. There were many evangelists who were taking the gospel message far and near and were seeing souls saved and baptised. New churches were being formed but teaching the Word of God was not being very successful. A number of ways were tried to deal with this real problem.

In three different centres the believers arranged to have short, intensive periods of study to cover systematically what the Scriptures taught. During these periods they were learning, so they said the students were at Bible School. This seemed a reasonable description, and so a 'Bible School' was formed in the north at Kashikishi, then one at Kawama and lastly one in Mambilima itself.

At Kashikishi a bookshop was built along with classrooms and living accommodation. The church gave themselves to this work, and it was great to see bricks moulded and burnt, then built into structures. They organised two months of teaching twice a year, and we were glad to be able to help the students.

At one stage we were teaching from the book of Exodus and had real difficulty describing the Tabernacle. One day there was no interpreter available so Margaret was called in to assist. Well Margaret is a nurse and for medical language she can trot it out fluently in Bemba, but it is different for tabernacle words! What about curtains, clasps and hooks, loops, couplings and taches of brass? - words not used at all frequently in Bemba! I learned something else that day - it is no easy matter to do the work of an interpreter!

The work at Kashikishi has been a real blessing. The church continued to be built up, and then it was great to help to build a High School where they now have 90 students taking grades 10, 11 and 12, all of which are now self sufficient.

Kawama had close associations with Mambilima over all the years. The original mission house there (first occupied by Mr George Lammond in 1929) was now in a state of disrepair and was in a dangerous condition. Mr Sims Mwansa lived there, a man with a heart for the work of God. He arranged for those interested in studying the Scriptures to meet on a monthly basis and thus the nucleus of another Bible School was formed. Every month three days of one week were set aside to systematically teach the Bible.

These were encouraging times when for six hours each day for the three days, around 20 believers would sit and study the Word of God in depth. Later a bookshop was built and then a classroom and some basic accommodation for the students.

At Mambilima also they commenced in a small way but developed a method that suited the believers. They met for a month twice a year, then moved on to two months twice a year. This group used different venues and classrooms on the mission. Around twelve students came to this teaching programme. Different teachers were involved including Alan Park, Jean-Luc Hainaut and Charles Muyembe.

Each school was responsible for the administration of its own course. The churches who were sending students were to help with the supply of food, and the students paid something toward their keep, being given breakfast, lunch and supper if resident. But sometimes the supply did not match what was needed. On completion the students were expected to share what they had learned with those in their own churches. It has been good to find now that a number of able teachers of the Word came from these groups of students.

Another group of people which we identified as needing help were the Sunday School teachers. With so many teaching aids available back in Scotland it was a surprise to find so little to stimulate interest. So we arranged a number of teaching days in different centres for the teachers, most of whom were men. Most of the ladies on leaving school, get married, have families and do not keep up their reading skills.

One of our first tasks was to make simple chalk boards. We cut appropriate sized pieces of cardboard from the boxes which came from Medical Missionary News. Black chalk-board paint was applied and chalk purchased – how basic but effective!

Then there were sessions on lesson preparation, suitable illustration and delivery. We taught them how to make their own flannel graphs with a piece of cloth over the board, drawing and cutting out pictures; then staple a square piece of sand paper onto the picture and stick it onto the cloth that way. With almost no money at their disposal we had to be ingenious as well as frugal!

Later on a supply of "real" flannel graph material was sent to us from John Ritchie Ltd in Scotland and we had the joy of teaching the skills of using it. After one such a lesson one child ran home and excitedly announced to her mother they had "television at Sunday School today"!

The whole area of learning through play was something else we introduced. This was a new concept to most of the would-be teachers. As some basic games were taught to them we had great fun and many a laugh. It was a lovely way to get to know the teachers and break down barriers. Margaret and I used to love giving these sessions and enjoying their *inshima* and whatever else that went with it!

Literature work was also dear to our heart as it had been over the years to those who had gone before us. There never seemed to be a constant and reliable supply of Bemba Bibles. Geoff Rushton has been a great help in negotiating with the Zambian Bible Society permission to reprint these Bibles: 20,000 copies were printed in South Korea but sold out very quickly, and another supply is already in the pipeline.

Many trips were made up the valley to set up a bookstall - many books and Bibles sold that way, also copies of English Bibles were sold to High School children for their religious studies.

In addition to Bibles we sold dictionaries, concordances and Study Bibles. The one commentary that has been of the greatest use is "The Believer's Bible Commentary" by Wm MacDonald. This is written in a style of English language which is easy to understand. All such helps have been sold at heavily subsidised prices to make them affordable to the level of poverty in village situations. Through these, many dear Christians have had their faith in God strengthened, and have been more able to teach the faith to others. We are grateful for the help of Echoes of Service, Every Day Publications and Lord's Work Trust in providing us with Bibles, books and teaching materials.

Wherever we went we would take literature and Gospels for distribution. These are always joyfully accepted by everyone - except on one occasion when offering one to a policeman.

He said, "This is not what I want, I want a BBC!" What is this he wants? we thought. Is he looking for a radio? No, he wanted a Believer's Bible Commentary! He was an elder in one of the churches.

Opportunity arose to produce the Bemba New Testament in a new format, on a solar powered i-pod by Megavoice. The New Testament was taken from recordings on tapes to CDs and then sent to Israel where it was transferred onto this little solar powered device. The quality of the spoken word is clear and accurate. It is a very useful tool for those who cannot read or see, or have little money for batteries. It also helps those who have recently learned to read to get their pronunciation right. So far 400 of these useful devices have found a home among Bemba speakers in this part of Zambia.

Another area of our service has been to assist many congregations to renew their church buildings. This was done by first encouraging them to do the work of making bricks and firing them in a kiln. Then we supplied them with cement, and local men built the hall. The congregation then collected wood for rafters and help was given to buy iron sheeting for the roof. This has enabled the replacement of many buildings that were dilapidated and falling down.

In the village of Mambilima itself the Mulundu church building was too small. So what they did was to build the shell of a larger building round about their existing structure. This took a number of years but eventually it was complete and the old decaying building was removed from inside! The foundation of this new building was laid in 2004 and now that it is completed they have a nice new hall to meet in.

Over these years it has been our joy to serve the Lord in such a variety of ways. His name has been magnified in this part of rural Zambia and His kingdom has been extended. We feel privileged to have been a cog integrated into one of the many wheels of work begun and continued by others mentioned in previous chapters. This humbles us, but also gratifies us to have been used in His service.

CHAPTER 24

Faithful Friends

During all these years at Mambilima we found those whom we grew to love in the Lord, and who remained faithful to us in the work they did. We would be unable to mention every one of them, but some do give us great pleasure even as we remember them now.

Charles Muyembe and his wife Grace have lived in the village all their life. One day he told me about the large mango tree at the foot of his garden and said it had been planted by his father. He speaks good English, and does it slowly and deliberately. He is the same when speaking Bemba so that even I can understand most of what he is saying.

Charles's hair is always in place, and he is always neat and well presented. He has a very wide extended family and is regularly off to far away places to attend a funeral as is the custom. As chairman of the hospital Board of Management he laboriously conducted the meetings. Characteristically after each item had been discussed and agreed he would say, "Progress," but for me it was so slow!

He is a faithful and loyal elder in the church, who gave many words of wisdom to the believers and to ourselves also. Charles has a good knowledge of the Bible and is a capable teacher who often assisted at the Bible School.

Sande Nsabaula and his wife Bupe (meaning Gift) were our

near neighbours in the village. At present he is 78 years of age. He was a school teacher until he retired in 1988, after which he went out with the Word of God into the villages as an evangelist. His mode of travel was his bicycle onto which he would pack his bag and books. Usually he would leave on a Friday and return on Tuesday or later. I asked him one day how many churches he had planted; he said there were fourteen. These were scattered over a wide area and some a great distance away.

Not only did Sande plant churches but he followed up the work and saw them well established. He had a great love for the backslider and would go to great lengths to seek and find them. When eating with him you could be sure that he would always ask for salt - which he seemed to need in an extra large amounts!

Bupe was active in the women's work and over the years she had worked with Cathie Arthur. They had their sewing class and this has continued to the present. Sande and Bupe have raised a large family which are a credit to them - Kaoma and Chisensele are both accountants and their daughters are teachers.

Sauti Chikoyi was the Head Teacher at the Mambilima School until he retired. He and his wife Eunice worked hard for the mission and for the church. They had only one son who went to Bulgaria and they lost contact with him until last year, but they had a large extended family whom they educated. He was a good teacher of the scriptures, able to expound clearly the Word of God. He suffered from asthma which curtailed his sphere of service, but he too was a very reliable member of the school Board of Management. As we are writing this, this dear brother has been called home to heaven.

Elliot Kamkomba was an elder in the Mulundu church in the village. He was an old worthy with whom we had many happy discussions. When we supplied him with a suit, he asked for a shirt to go with it, then he needed a tie, next socks and shoes, and last of all he asked for a coat to complete the outfit. The next time we saw him he was preaching at a funeral in the village. The sun was blazing hot as usual but there he was complete with overcoat sounding forth the Word! If you have it you need to show it!

Four Old Worthies at Mambilima, 2009

Reuben Kaoma and Francis Chikonde are two evangelists who have worked together in the spread of the gospel. Reuben was born in the district and is married, with seven children. Having been saved and baptised he was commended to the work of an evangelist in 1986. Francis comes from the Northern Province and after trusting the Saviour and being baptised he was commended to work as an evangelist on the Copperbelt in 1972. He is married to Charity and they have been blessed with eight children.

We first met Francis in the early days, and he was slowly becoming unable to do very much work. He had a massive goitre the size of a football. What could be done? The hospital would not operate to excise it and he was slowly being strangled to death. Margaret was seeing a brilliant surgeon, Dr Lebaq, at a clinic in Mukushi. He had pictures on his wall of patients from whom he had successfully removed equally large goitres. We spoke to him about Francis and he agreed to see him.

The outcome was that he agreed to operate. Afterwards he said, "Well, when I started the necessary surgery I was worried about Francis's vocal chords as he was a preacher, but as I went on I started to worry about his life! The growth tendrils reached down into his chest and were beginning to strangle his heart." He confessed later that he wished he had never started the operation, but God gave him strength and ability to complete it. Francis recovered successfully, and continues to work in his garden and goes on preaching as an evangelist.

Both Francis and Reuben went to study the Bible more deeply by taking a one year course at Samfya Bible School. This gave them more in-depth knowledge and prepared them better for future service.

Reuben and Francis have worked together in the Luapula and Northern Provinces, and also in the Democratic Republic of Congo. Together they have worked with a number of missionaries and have seen 24 churches planted. They have also helped ten churches that were in need of encouragement to burn more brightly for God.

There are others in the valley whom we can name as they have helped us in our ministry. Ba Jonas Katontoka was a Luanza man who was at Kashikishi, an old man whose advice and wise counsel we greatly valued. He was a capable teacher of the Word and although it was not easy for us to communicate with each other we seemed to think in the same way. His son Puta is a hard working evangelist among the forest peoples and on the islands of the Luapula.

Daniel Mukuka and his wife Felicity were good friends. He worked for the Zambian Electric Company and was a member of the Mambilima School Board. They live at Musonda Falls where the church is involved in effective outreach. They have a real heart for the Lord's Work. It was good to be a help to their family.

Gershom works as an evangelist in the Musonda area. Equipped with a bicycle and a tent away he goes into the villages. These evangelists are self supporting, depending on the Lord to supply their needs. Most of them are grateful for a wife who looks after their gardens and grows crops to feed their families. It has been a privilege to assist many of them to build a house and help to educate their children. The Lord has promised to supply all our needs, and theirs, according to His riches in glory in Christ Jesus (Philippians 4.19).

Kennedy Chikonde is a young man who was brought up in the village, and lives nearby with his wife and family. Kennedy went to Mansa and learned the skills of carpentry. Now he works in the village and on the mission as a capable carpenter, a most dependable lad who is also trustworthy. He is a "committee" man and is on conference, Bible School and whatever committee. He is an elder in a small church on the outskirts of the village and has been a good friend to us over the years.

It is good to go down memory lane like this and recall those with whom we have laboured in the Lord, brothers and sisters in Christ who have little of this world's goods, yet have the greatest gift of all in Jesus Christ our Lord. Like Paul they can say "I can do everything through Christ who pours His strength into me" (Philippians 4.13).

Over the years it has been a privilege to work with SHAREZambia. This group of believers is based in Lusaka and is the Zambian arm of SHAREAfrica. Their aim is to assist churches in different areas of Zambia, to try to get believers out of the poverty trap and become self supporting and sustaining. They have been attempting this in a variety of ways. In 2010 we discussed the possibility of getting a project started at Mambilima involving growing and marketing groundnuts. This commenced in 2011 and now in 2012 they expect to harvest their first crops. The nuts will be bought, transported to Lusaka for processing, and the families growing the nuts will be paid for their work. We hope that such projects can be expanded to help more believers achieve some independence of living. We know that the love of God can be manifested in many ways.

* * * * * * *

Thus the work of God in this province continues to move forward as it has done for over a hundred years. The mighty Luapula River keeps flowing on unchanged towards the sea, the huge Rock formations remain as steady as ever, while those who are the precious Redeemed of the Lord change with every new generation. We have seen in these pages how many hear and believe and go on to tell others.

The Word of the Lord endures forever. Our Lord said, "Heaven and earth shall pass away, but my words shall not pass away" (Matthew 24.35).

Epilogue

What a journey this has been as we have traced developments over 114 years at Mambilima and district! Great changes have taken place, and the one big factor in all these changes is the power of God to make men and women new creatures in Christ Jesus. There have been social changes in the country, advances in modern technology have had their effect, but the biggest change has come from the inside of a person due to a change of heart.

Dan Crawford has left this paragraph on record:

> "Black as coal, every one of them; yet, after all diamonds are made of soot, albeit the how, when, and where of the miracle we may not know. Moreover, it doth not yet appear what this black land of ours shall be, but we know that God with swift silent steps can make and give the crystallising touch that makes the diamond flash out of the quondam soot. "Rags" the Arab calls our black parishioners, forgetful of the fact that rags make the whitest paper; so what man can do in the paper line, surely God can surpass in souls."

We have seen the change from cannibalism to living peacefully with one's neighbour, from illiteracy to being able to read and write, moving from building with wood and clay to brick and cement, from grass roofs to those of tin and tiles, from tribal medicine to scientific treatments and surgery. Men and women have passed from spiritual death to eternal life, as did those of

Thessalonica who long ago "turned to God from idols to serve the living and true God" (1 Thessalonians 1.9).

Fred Stanley Arnot visited Mambilima on his journey home to Scotland. He sat round the camp fire and ate the native bread or mush and venison. He spoke to them of the Lord's first coming, of His death and resurrection, and of the gospel which was preached all over the ancient world. Then came long years of silence as far as Africa was concerned. But now East, West, North and South, people are hearing what their fathers and grandfathers had never heard. People are believing the message and now are waiting for the Lord's second coming to take his people away from this world.

As they sat round the fire a young convert stood up and read the scripture, "Blessed are the eyes which see the things that you see, ... and hear those things which you hear" (Luke 10.23-24). In a spirit of thanksgiving he lifted their spirits, rejoicing that in "God's mercy the gospel had been brought to them, poor Ba-Bemba sinners".

Arnot observed that "in all stations our brethren have great plans and projects for the extension of the work; and so it ought to be, and ever will be, if we are serving in communion with the Master Servant. As the ship can never overtake the ocean horizon, so the missionary's hands and feet can never reach as far as his eyes and heart".

As we ourselves now move on, having served in our time with those lovely people and performed what the Lord gave us strength to do, we pass on the baton in the great Christian race to our Zambian brothers and sisters. By God's grace and help they will take the work forward and build on what has already been achieved.

In a day soon to come, around the throne of the Lamb of God in heaven a countless multitude will gather from every nation, kindred, tongue, and people to sing the praise and glory due to His name. We rejoice that among them there will be thousands from the Luapula valley, and together we will fall at the feet of our Lord and Saviour and cry, "Thou art worthy, O Lord!"

Amen and Amen.

Appendix 1

SIGNIFICANT EVENTS IN THE HISTORY
OF MAMBILIMA MISSION
1897 - 2012

(During British colonial times Mambilima was called Johnston Falls, named after the great administrator Sir Harry Johnston. Before 1963 Zambia was Northern Rhodesia, named after Cecil Rhodes)

1897   Mr and Mrs Dan Crawford make their first visit to Chief Mulundu's village called Mambilima. Dan Crawford and Henry Pomeroy visit Johnston Falls.

1898   After trouble with Paramount Chief Kazembe, Pomeroy allowed to settle.

1899   Henry Pomeroy has to leave through illness; Mr and Mrs Anderson (his sister) arrive.

1900   The Andersons leave Johnston Falls because of illness.

1901   Bwana Kiana established a *Boma* at Johnston Falls. Mr and Mrs Dugald Campbell arrive and take over the work. William Lammond pays his first visit.

1902   James Anton arrives. The Campbells go to Luanza for birth of child, where Mrs Campbell dies. William Lammond pays a second visit to Johnston Falls accompanied by William White who stays on.

1903   Campbell and White move to Chipundu where White
        starts school work. Lammond pays a third visit to
        Johnston Falls.

1905   Mr and Mrs Lammond arrive and take over at
        Johnston Falls.

1906   Mrs Lammond dies. William Lammond leaves and
        walks to west coast while Mr Campbell continues.
        Sleeping Sickness first appears at Kasenga.

1907   Mr Patterson joins Mr Campbell.

1908   W Lammond remarries and returns Johnston Falls,
        along with A E Shapland and Miss H Copenet.

1909   Campbell off on leave intending to return and open
        up work in Usho country.

1910   Bwingi Milonga begins; Sleeping Sickness rampant.
        The whole Luapula valley depopulated, moving to
        Kaleba, much suffering and death. Mulundu's people
        go to Mofwe; Mr Patterson goes home sick.
        George W Sims joins the work at Kaleba.

1911   George Sims goes to help at Bwingi. Much building at
        Kaleba.

1912   Miss Nesbet joins the work for a year.

1913   Mr and Mrs George Lammond arrive.

1914   Outbreak of World War I - many men away carrying
        for the army.

1915   Mr and Mrs Sims return to Kaleba after leave.

1916   Bemba New Testament and Psalms is produced by W Lammond

1918   The Sims go to Mwenso wa Nsoka. William Lammond and Dora return from leave.

1919   Influenza hits the district, much illness, many deaths, much suffering and hardship.

1920   Mr and Mrs Thomas Higgins begin at Mubende; Mr and Mr James Anton begin at Chibambo.
First general conference held at Kaleba.
Mr William D. McKenzie comes to Kaleba.

1922   Ban on the Luapula is lifted; much rejoicing as the people return to build houses and cultivate.
During 1910 - 1922 much work done at Kaleba; a large hall built and churches established at Mumbolo, Salanga and Mulumbwa; also many primitive schools started.

1924   Mr and Mrs John McKenzie come to Johnston Falls and relieve the Lammonds. More than 120 are enrolled as believers; a church planted at Kashiba.

1925   Mr and Mrs Lammond return along with Miss Beatrice Fraser, a trained nurse. Medical work begins in a more organised way.

1926   Mr Charles E Stokes, a school master, joins the work at Johnston Falls; school work put on a proper basis. (Later on a teacher training centre at Johnston Falls continued until the Government rationalized training.)
Miss Ethel Woolnough arrives, giving the girls a trained teacher for the first time; left the valley for health reasons in 1943.

A bad year for lions, several people killed.

1927   A second church established at Mukomansala.

1930   Church begins at Lubundu.

1931   Jubilee year of Mr F S Arnot. Mr Lesley Barham visits
        and stays for two years. Mr Paterson visits and helps
        with the new senior school (later killed while
        elephant hunting). Mr Charles S Swan visits and lays
        commemoration stone in new school. Churches begin
        at Kabundafyela and Nkomba.

1932   Churches begin at Mulonga, Matente and Chalwe,
        and another at Matente following a mutually agreed
        move from Kashiba.

1935   Church at Sicibangu begins.

1936   Mr Stokes marries Miss Ruth Pickering amidst great
        rejoicing.
        Another church begins at Kolala's village.

1937   Mr Ray Smith arrives and does excellent work until
        1942 when he became Principal of the Hodgson
        Training College.
        Mr and Mrs L Barham get married. Dr and Mrs
        Stanley Mason also have their official wedding here
        (the religious one at Chibambo).

1940   The Chisheta church begins.
        School for the blind begins at Johnston Falls (with
        only 4 pupils, in 1958 there were 44).

1942   The Church at Lupito begins.

1944   Miss Meryl J Shepherd and Miss Mary Noeline

Stockdale join the work. Gospel Hall is burnt down by a madman; three lions killed which were terrorising the district.

1946   Miss Elizabeth M Shepherd arrives. The church at Mupeta begins.

1948   Miss Winifred R Wagland joins the work, then goes to Pweto after first furlough (later she became Mrs William Rew).
Mr and Mrs Norman Budge arrive; Mr and Mrs Stokes leave after Mr Stokes' severe illness.
Miss Fraser leaves; Miss Noeline Stockdale takes over the hospital.

1949   Miss Cathie E Arthur and also Mr Archie M Ross arrive.

1950   Mr W Lammond celebrates his Jubilee. Mr and Mrs Budge leave the valley for health reasons.

1951   Mr and Mrs Ross are married at Lwela.

1952   Mr Anton dies at Chibambo; also Mrs Lammond after a long illness.

1953   Mr W Lammond and Miss E M Shepherd were married.
Kamfwelele church begins. Trouble in the valley over fishing rights, armed forces take over for a time.
Rosses go to Luwingu.

1954   Mr and Mrs James Ford and family arrive.

1956   Churches at Kanyemba and at Tangwa commence. The Bemba Bible first produced.

1957   New block for hospital begins but unfinished due to delay in Government assistance.
        Church begins at Bunda's village on the upper Lungo largely due to the work of Katala and later of Joseph Mwansa.

1958   The year of the Diamond Jubilee.
        At Nacisaka the 21st local church in the area commences.
        Mr and Mrs J F McKenzie, Mr and Mrs G O Ratteray, Mr and Mrs G M Lammond, Mr and Mrs A E Morse help during W L's furlough.
        Miss L B Gordon and Miss A E Fulton help during Miss Fraser's leave.
        Dr P Dixon gives unstinting labour and saves the life of William Lammond.

1960   Dr Keir Howard and his wife Dorothy join the work as doctor and nurse/midwife, until 1964 when they move up country.

1960   Miss Irene Mann joins the staff and gives valuable service as a nurse and midwife until 1965 when she leaves to marry Mr Alan Gammon and moved to South Africa.

1964   Zambia achieves independence. Johnston Falls renamed Mambilima.

1968   William Lammond passed into the Lord's presence.

1970   Miss Morag Anthony joins the work until 1984.

1974   Miss Margaret Jarvis is at Mambilima until 1981 when she had to leave because of repeated severe malaria attacks. She returns to Mambilima in 1998 as Mrs Margaret Muir.

1979   Joyce Ramsay came and served until 1981.

1980   Three short term nurses gave service until 1982.

1981   John Walters gave some months of service.

1983   Mark Davies arrived in February.

1984   Miss Noeline Stockdale retires from medical work,
        but continues a book and visitation ministry in the
        villages until finally retiring to the UK in 1988.
        Miss Shirley Thomson came in November 1984;
        married Mark Davies in 1986; they moved to Samfya
        in 1991.

1985   Anita Crozier and Margaret King (now Mrs Margaret
        Rutter) arrive and serve for one year as nurses.

1987   Dr Martin and Naomi Cooper join the work, with
        their two sons, until 1993.
        Miss Cathie Arthur retires from medical work then
        takes up visitation and giving material help in
        surrounding villages.

1989   Mr and Mrs Ken Hatcher arrive to work respectively
        in administration and as a nurse and midwife,
        retiring in 1995.
        Mr and Mrs Rod Boatman also arrive, working
        respectively in maintenance and building work, and
        as a nurse and midwife, until 1991.

1990   June Hartley came in October.

1996   Miss Jean and Miss Ann Frances joined the work for
        one year.

1997   Mr and Mrs Scott Kitchen at Mambilima for language

study for a year.
Miss Cathie Arthur retired from her work at
Mambilima (there since 1949).

1998   Mr and Mrs Robert Muir arrive and are involved in
       all aspects of administration until their return to the
       UK in 2006; since then continuing to help in
       administration, visiting normally twice a year.

Appendix 2

MAMBILIMA BUILDING PROGRAMMES

1922 – 1997

1923	Hall for local church with large tree supports
1931	School building - commemoration stone laid by Mr Swan
1932	Church building with brick pillars and iron roof
1957	A 14 bed ward built at hospital
1958	Another 14 bed ward built
1959	A new block built at the hospital which includes

      - a delivery room
      - a post natal ward with seven beds and seven cots
      - dispensary
      - examination room
      - office

1970 – 75

A U-shaped block built by Mission Medic Air which included

      - children's ward, with 11 beds and toilet and shower
      - under 5s clinic
      - X-Ray room
      - laundry room
      - kitchen and food store

1980 – 85

A new block for children's wards, examination rooms, under 5s room, and antenatal rooms
(This block was built by Mr Roberts from Bermuda giving better and larger facilities. Earlier buildings converted for other uses.)

1987   Mortuary

1998 – 2012

Hospital

1998   Perimeter concrete wall fence with entrance gate

1999   Four houses for staff

2000   Original hospital administration block demolished
Foundation work commenced for Operating Theatre
(This was to be a community project but did not get very far.)

2003   Murray Out-patient Department - waiting room, two consulting rooms, a treatment room, a pharmacy and a records office.

2005   Operating Theatre built

2006   Two wards for women built, the McQueen Wards

2007   Two wards for men built
New Laboratory built

2008   Accommodation for relatives provided, a block with 10 rooms
A house for staff rebuilt
A dental room built

2009   Nutrition ward with four beds plus a kitchen
Incinerator built
Three more staff houses built

Schools

2004	Brass Tacks team at Mambilima
	-new school built
	-dining hall doubled in size
	-foundation slab for a new church building laid
2006	Bore Hole for water and pump installed
2007	House for Head Teacher of High School
2009	Three classrooms, offices and storerooms for the High School
	Another house for staff
	Conversion of unused building to a hostel for 20 High School boys and a dormitory for house parent
2010	A hostel for 16 High School girls and a dormitory for house parent

Mission

2008	CMML Conference Site
	- two blocks of 10 rooms, one for men and the other for women
	- two blocks with toilets and washrooms
	- house for security guard
2010	New water tanks installed

Bibliography

This is a brief selection of material which can give more information and additional background to the missionary work described in this book.

Baker, E *The Life and Explorations of F S Arnot*, Seely, Service and Co., Ltd. 38 Great Russell Street, London, 1921

Barham, R *Remember your Leaders – imitate their faith*, 40 pages (messages given at the Christian Brethren (CMML) Centenary Conference 24th August 1998). African Christian Books, P.O. Box 90376, Luanshya, Zambia 1998

Campbell, Dugald F.R.G.S. *Blazing Trails in Bantuland*, 228 pages. Pickering and Inglis, Glasgow, 1932

Campbell, Dugald F.R.G.S. *In the Heart of Bantuland*, 313 pages. Pickering and Inglis, Glasgow

Crawford, Dan *Thinking Black*, 458 pages. Morgan and Scott, 12 Paternoster Buildings, E.C. London, 1912; Reprinted by John Ritchie Ltd., Kilmarnock, 2009

Crawford, Dan *Back to the Long Grass, My Link with Livingstone*, 373 pages. Hodder and Stoughton Ltd, London

Ellis, James J *Dan Crawford of Luanza*, 160 pages. John Ritchie, Kilmarnock, Scotland

Fulton, A E   *From Forest Track to Tarmac*, Bala, North Wales, Dragon Books, 1970

Goodman, M   *A Central African Jubilee 1881 – 1931*, Pickering and Inglis, Glasgow

Muir, Robert   *You Shall Go Out With Joy*, 135 pages. John Ritchie Ltd, Kilmarnock, Scotland, 2010

Mutenda, Kovina L K   *A History of Christian Brethren in Zambia*, 198 pages. Christian Resource, P.O. Box11235, Chingola Zambia, 2002

Stunt, W T   *Turning the World Upside Down*, 661 pages. Upperton Press, Upperton Gardens, Eastbourne, Sussex, 1972

Tatford, Fredk. A   *Light over the Dark Continent*, 547 pages. Echoes Publications, 1 Widcombe Crescent, Bath, Avon, 1984

Some Magazines which have given helpful contributions to this story:

Echoes of Service. Annual Bound Copies, 1898 to 1996; Brethren Archives, Rylands University, Manchester

Horizon, p33, November 1965; *Lammond, Willie - Pioneer Missionary who laughed at death*

Links of Help, 1911 to 1918, Pickering and Inglis, 11 Bothwell Circus, Glasgow

Links of Help, Davos Mount, Buxton, Darbyshire; *Campbell, Dugald: Bembaland and Lake Bangweula, In Arnot's Footsteps*

Open Brethren (Christian Mission in Many Lands), Dictionary of African Christian Biography, 2010; Howard, J K *Lammond, William 1876 to 1968*

Wikipedia, the free encyclopedia, 2010; *Kazembe*

MAP OF ZAMBIA AND NEIGHBOURING COUNTRIES
showing places referred to in this book
(Taken by permission from *Light over the Dark Continent* p 416, F A Tatford;
Echoes of Service, Bath, 1984)